Life Rewritten

Life Rewritten

Carrie KC West

Waterside Productions

www.carriekcwest.com

First Printing, 2025

ISBN-13: 978-1-962984-82-9 print edition
ISBN-13: 978-1-962984-83-6 ebook edition

Waterside Productions
2055 Oxford Ave
Cardiff, CA 92007
www.waterside.com

Life Rewritten / Carrie KC West – 1st ed.
Author Carrie KC West
Edited by Lisa Dale Norton, Jenn Brown, and Susan Crossman
Graphic Design by Kelly Pasholk, Wink Visual Arts

For the storyteller in each of us.

We are the story and the story is who we are.

Table of Contents

Introduction

The difference between your present self and your desired self hinges on a single, powerful element: the story you tell about yourself and your potential. How do I know this? Because I am living proof. In the chapters that follow, I will share how, through a deep understanding of life as a story, I transformed my existence from barely surviving to living a rich and fulfilling life brimming with every kind of abundance.

I had a rough start in life, though not in the way you might expect. I wasn't physically harmed or beaten, but what my parents did left even deeper scars: they ignored me. I remember Mom telling people that when I cried, I was put in a closet; when I was hungry, I had to wait until she felt like feeding me. I wasn't held, cradled, or comforted. To my newborn mind, I imagine that this isolation felt like solitary confinement. The impact of that neglect stayed with me for years.

Mom stopped ignoring me when I was about two years old. That's when she realized I could serve a purpose for her. She began to teach me, not through love, but through expectations. I became responsible for my baby sister, Tessa, who was born just before my second birthday. I gave Tessa her bottle and soothed her cries, all to keep Mom from getting upset. At a very early age, I learned that my needs were always secondary to others.

At night, I would lie awake, unable to sleep, until I discovered the comfort of storytelling. In my mind, I created rich tales of my "real" mom, who loved me and was searching for me. I knew she would rescue me from this life. Every night, I added a new chapter, imagining my real parents as loving, larger-than-life figures who would carry me away into a life of joy and comfort. Through these stories, I found peace, even at a young age.

That's the power of story. It carried me through some of my darkest moments, providing a place of calm when reality felt too harsh. As I grew, I searched for ways to make sense of my life—therapy, meditation, and countless self-help techniques were helpful. But the real breakthrough came when I was studying at the American Film Institute in my early thirties. Immersed in the art of storytelling, I saw clearly how the stories we write mirror the lives we lead. It brought my childhood bedtime stories into sharper focus, showing me the incredible connection between narrative and healing. Today, stories have become an important tool I use to assist my clients to create new lives for themselves.

MY APPROACH

Many books discuss personal narratives, and there is a branch of psychology devoted to them. What sets my work apart is its foundation in a deep understanding of the storytelling process. This goes beyond recognizing the importance of narrative by delving into the key story elements that reflect our deepest beliefs and desires.

THE CONCEPT OF LIFE AS A STORY

Our lives are stories, and like any great story, they can be rewritten to create the ending we seek. This book dives into the building blocks of storytelling, guiding you to reshape your narrative and reclaim authorship of your journey. Here's a preview of what's inside:

Themes and Motivations: Understanding the themes and motivations in your personal narrative is the first step in rewriting your story. By revealing and working with the themes that dominate your life, you can see how they influence your decisions and experiences.

Characters: Characters are the linchpin of every story. In personal stories, we often play both the protagonist and the supporting cast. Dissecting the roles and traits we embody has a far-reaching impact on our journey to fulfillment. This process allows us to redefine our character, grasp the influence of other characters, and make new choices that align with our goals and values.

Plot: The plot encompasses the patterns of reality, including the repeated challenges that throw you off course. Recognizing these patterns helps you anticipate obstacles and develop strategies to overcome them, transforming struggles into stepping-stones.

Point of View: While you are the author of your story, it is often filtered through perspectives shaped by past experiences and beliefs. You tell your story through the lens from which you perceive it. That's why the other people in your story will often describe the same events you experienced in a completely different way. Shifting your perspective can offer new insights and possibilities, helping you see your journey in a fresh light.

BRINGING YOUR STORY TO LIFE

Stories are an integral part of who we are. We live in a time of uncertainty, which amplifies stress and anxiety, especially now that so much is unknown. My approach inspires people and businesses to reimagine a way forward and envision what's possible. By framing the process of self-discovery as a story, I add an element of ease and intrigue. This approach alleviates the discomfort often associated with personal growth and brings a sense of levity and creativity to the journey.

YOUR JOURNEY BEGINS

I've included exercises in each chapter to help you dig into how different aspects of your story have shaped who you are today. For any part of your story that no longer works for who you want to be, remember - you have the power to change it. The pen is in your hand. Let's begin writing the new story of your extraordinary life.

A THOUGHT ABOUT JOURNALS

I strongly encourage you to keep a journal as you work through the exercises in this book. I've kept journals since I was a teenager. Although I sometimes cringe when I read them now, they always provide new insights, and often make me smile. Writing by hand helps me retain what I've learned. However, if you prefer, you can use a document on your computer or tablet to capture your innermost thoughts. The important thing is to create a space where you feel free to express whatever is happening for you at that moment.

STRUCTURE OF THE BOOK

Each chapter begins with a story from my life that covers the element presented. While the stories are true, I've changed the names of others involved to respect their privacy. After the story, I delve into the concept, providing depth and meaning. Each chapter closes with specific steps to bring the idea of storytelling alive in your own world.

In the coming chapters, I invite you to examine your story, redefine your narrative, and transform your life. By understanding and harnessing the power of storytelling, you can bridge the gap between your present self and your desired self, creating a life filled with purpose, abundance, and fulfillment.

Think of the stories you'll tell then.

For additional help, PDF downloads, resources and information on scheduling a private session, visit my website, carriekcwest.com, where you will find more ideas and support. For your convenience, please use the QR Code below:

1

Life as a Story

> Stop waiting! We are the authors of our lives. You write the story. You have no one to blame but yourself. If you want to change the circumstances, then change them. Only you can do it.
>
> — Ruth Ellingham, *Doc Martin*

October 1992, Hollywood, CA

The sun shone brightly through the large windows of the Fellows Lounge of the Warner Bros. building. The walls were covered with images from past films and student projects—some black and white, others full color—they humbled me and made me feel lucky to be included in such an elite institution. The air was thick with the history of the film industry. I could feel the energy of those who had come before me, Terrence Malick, Carl Franklin, Jon Avnet, Katherine Helmond, James Horner, Amy Heckerling… the list was long and would grow over the years. I sat with a group of Fellows talking about our scripts for our first film project. We were all new to the program and just forming relationships that we all hoped would last through long, industrious careers in the film industry. The people we met there, we were told, could be the people we worked with for years to come. It was exciting and scary.

The American Film Institute (AFI) was an icon. I couldn't believe my luck in attending it. It was almost ten years since my dad died, leaving me feeling alone and betrayed. His death took me to the absolute lowest part of my life. Months after he died, I hit rock bottom, relying on beer and nachos to get me through the day. But reaching that point pushed me into finally doing something with my life. I started therapy, went to healing groups, practiced meditation and attended metaphysical workshops. I did anything I could to make sense of the psychological and emotional pain that left me adrift in life. The idea of even applying to the AFI was more of a dare than a belief that I could get accepted.

But as I sat in that sunny room on that day with people who would one day be recognized names in the industry, I didn't know that I was about to understand my life in an intense way. I listened as the group of future directors and producers, writers and cinematographers sat around talking about stories, the themes, characters, arcs, and plots, all critical to "get right" as we prepared our first projects. Something gnawed at the back of my mind, "Characters – antagonists/protagonists; Themes – Love wins/hurts/sucks; the story arc, moving through events and changing to meet the final challenge…" And then, an acute sense of knowing came over me, an "A Ha!" moment of grand awareness. My life was a story. A complex, undeniably shitty story, but a story. I had characters, themes, and plots that repeated themselves more than I liked. If that's the case, maybe, I thought, I could look at it all, just like we're doing here and maybe, I could change my story just like we're rewriting our projects now.

STORIES AND HEALING

In my work, when I meet a new client unfamiliar with my process, I start by asking, "What is a story?" Most people mention movies or books, which are correct. Then I follow up with, "What is your story?" The answers are usually vaguer and more disconnected, which makes sense. People rarely think of their lives as unfolding stories. Instead, they focus on the present moment, their decisions, and their immediate responses.

In the opening scene above, I share how I came to embrace the concept of "life as a story." Since that meeting at AFI, I have examined my story and transformed my life into something of my own creation.

Understanding life as a story is crucial because it structures the process of healing emotional wounds and creating a life of your choosing in the following ways:

Purpose and Meaning: Viewing your life as a story or narrative allows you to identify recurring themes, challenges you've overcome, and goals you've achieved. It changes how you look at your life, which can empower and alleviate feelings of emptiness, replacing them with a sense of purpose and direction.

Understanding Life's Path: When you look at life as a story, you discover past experiences that shaped the person you are today. This shift in perspective fosters greater self-compassion.

Motivation and Goal Setting: Stories are about overcoming obstacles and achieving goals. Framing your life this way can motivate you to act and strive for a better future in your own narrative.

The Future: Seeing life as a story allows you to see the future and the possibilities with more hope and excitement. It becomes easier to believe in a happy ending and do something great for yourself, your family, and the world.

WHAT IS A STORY?

A story is a series of events shared to entertain, inform, or convey a message or moral lesson. People often tell stories to connect with others, find common ground, and get to know each other. Stories entertain, spark curiosity, and evoke emotions. They shape a sense of identity and belonging. Stories reflect cultural values, traditions, and history, creating shared experiences across generations.

Storytelling is woven into every aspect of life. But how did stories become so ingrained in reality? To understand this, you need to look at how the brain works. Brains are hardwired to respond to stories, striving to make sense of randomness by recognizing and accepting patterns. These patterns often revolve around the people you encounter, who are seen as characters in your personal stories. From infancy, you absorb information and lessons from the stories told by parents, family members, and people in your community, all of which shape your understanding of the world and your place in it. Thus, the concept of "story" naturally supports and leverages the brain's functions.

In your experience of reality, you subconsciously organize events into narratives. This helps you remember experiences, spot similarities, and make sense of the world around you.

THE PLOT THICKENS

Personal stories set you apart from others. The stories you're exposed to and the ones you tell about yourself shape your identity. They define who you are, what you value, and how you fit into the world. When you tell your story, you're essentially doing a self-check. Whenever you share a personal tale, you are saying, "I'm a good person," or "I made a mistake, but I learned from it." The goal is to get the listener to relate to you, find you trustworthy, and feel like they know you. You want them to nod along, showing they understand and maybe have had similar experiences.

Sometimes, holding onto your story is a way to justify your actions and seek acceptance. It's fascinating how personal narratives are fluid and ever-changing, evolving with each telling based on the situation and audience and bringing new experiences and insights.

From this perspective, rewriting your story becomes an engaging and enjoyable process. Viewing your life from this vantage point, you uncover the values and challenges that have shaped your life and help you see how others view you. This new awareness empowers you to make choices aligned with your dreams. You start to see your past struggles as challenges you've overcome. Reflecting on past events from your current standpoint can be incredibly rewarding, fostering a sense of achievement. You become the heroine of your own narrative, taking charge of your life and crafting chapters with a happy ending.

Plot Points

To Recap:

- Your brain constantly seeks patterns to make sense of the world. Stories provide a framework for this, using the "story arc" concept that helps you make sense of events and situations.
- When you engage with stories, areas of the brain activate. This is thought to be partly due to "mirror neurons," which fire when we observe actions or emotions in others.
- Your brain anticipates what will happen next in a story. In your personal narratives, it fills in gaps when information is missing, often leading to incorrect conclusions that can negatively impact your life.
- Stories that evoke both positive and negative emotions are the most memorable. The emotional connection strengthens the neural pathways tied to the information, making it stick.

What's Your Story?

At the end of each chapter, I take you through the process of rewriting your story. I recommend getting a journal or setting up a document on your computer to take notes and follow along.

Start thinking about your life as a story and consider the following steps:

Step 1: Imagine Your Life as a Movie

When you think of a movie, it has a beginning, a middle, and an end.

- Now think of your life and ask yourself the following questions:
  - — The beginning of your life typically runs from the day you were born until you're eighteen. Think about how those years unfolded for you. Are any events or memories particularly important to you?
  - — The middle of a movie is the longest section. The middle of your life story typically stretches from the beginning of adulthood to where you are today.
  - — See how this section is different from the beginning, full of all the adventures you've encountered.
  - — You probably experienced many endings in your life. Can you think of a couple and how they signified the beginning of a new chapter?
- Think about some key points as you start to see your life as a story.

Step 2: Identify Patterns

As you think about the events in your life, look for any recurring themes and behaviors. Is there something that seems to come up "all the time?" For example, in my life, I frequently found myself having unexpected expenses just as I was starting to save some money. I remembered thinking that there was some gremlin that caused my car to break down or some health crisis to arise just as I made a deposit into my savings account. I'll dig into the patterns in other chapters. For now, think about the circumstances that occur repeatedly.

Step 3: Identify Key Characters

Who are the characters in your life movie? I've included a chapter on characters called "Heroes and Villains" later, but for now, start thinking about the significant people in your life.

Step 4: Reflect on Challenges

Every life has challenges to varying degrees. What were some of the challenges you faced at various ages? How did you overcome these obstacles? What impact did they have on your development?

Each of these areas will be discussed fully in later chapters. This exercise will set the tone for this journey. Take note of what you discover in your initial responses to the questions. These observations are the beginnings of your life story. By identifying key patterns and challenges, you'll gain insight into how this story has shaped your narrative—the tale you tell yourself and others about who you are.

2

Your Origin Story

We accept the reality of the world we find ourselves in.

— Christof, *The Truman Show*

October 1956

It was 1:00 a.m. on a Monday morning—October 22nd, to be precise. When Mom told me years later about that night I imagined the quiet darkness of her bedroom. It was a small bedroom filled with the double bed she shared with Dad and a large dresser facing it on the opposite wall. Both were hand-me-downs from Dad's older sister. Aunt Tessa gave the furniture to them when she moved to Florida after her husband had enough of the cold winters in Pittsburgh.

A year earlier, Mom and Dad had moved into their new house on Outlook Drive, which was a perfect size for a family of four: Mom, Dad, and my brother and sister. It was a small home with three tiny bedrooms, but it would work for them.

Mom wasn't sleeping well. Even though it was a cool October evening, sweat consumed her. Her huge pregnant belly, close to term, was more than uncomfortable. Her back hurt, and her ankles and feet were swollen. She wanted me, this baby inside of her, out. She said that she cursed herself for letting this happen again—this pregnancy. But who was she kidding, she told me. She put all her hopes on me, this baby inside her—hopes for her marriage, her future… and so far, it had been a bust. My dad, James, was lately even more distant with her than he had been after his mother died. Mom said that he was furious when she told him she was pregnant. "Get rid of it," he told her. Mom refused. "Another fucking mouth to feed," he cursed. Mom said that she was surprised. She thought he liked being a father.

Mom thought of her mother-in-law and the anguish her death caused my dad. Mom told me she hated my grandmother for the hold she had on him. Mom would spit three times to avoid a curse for speaking ill of the dead. It wasn't my grandmother Carrie's fault James was so devoted to her. Still, Mom wished she'd never stopped using her diaphragm. Mom said she hated the baby that was me, and I wasn't even here yet.

Her water broke as if I, the child inside, heard her call to get out of her womb. She poked at her snoring husband. He grumbled. "Get up. I need a ride to the hospital." He got up, reluctantly dressed, and went outside in the chill October morning. He started the car. Mom waddled into the passenger seat, and they drove in silence to Allegheny General, twenty minutes away, while Mom grimaced every time a contraction came. She thought about her two older children, sleeping in their beds, and cursed again for putting herself through what was going to be a long day of pushing and pain. She was tired, she said, not just from the pregnancy but also from her life. They drove in silence to Allegheny General Hospital, the sound of the car the only noise to fill the empty space between them. Dad left her at the entrance, not bothering to walk her to Admissions, and returned home to his warm bed.

Mom made her way slowly to the desk. The nurses were kind, she said. They took great care of her, getting her a wheelchair and finding a bed for her in the maternity wing. The staff responded pretty quickly. At that early Monday morning hour, there wasn't much activity. Plus, her water did break, and her contractions were already seven minutes apart.

After twelve hours of pushing and feeling ripped apart, Mom said I emerged out of her body and into the world. The nurse held me while the doctor snipped the umbilical cord. The nurse handed me to Mom. Mom, tired from the labor, took one look at me and said, "Get that disgusting thing away from me!" Mom said that she turned her head away while the nurse quickly wrapped me in a blanket, put me in a plastic crib, and sent me to the nursery, where a different nurse cleaned and wrapped me in another warm blanket. I was placed in a row with other newborns in a bright room. I had no idea where I was, who I was, or what was happening.

Mom said that after they took me away, she finally slept. They brought me to her sometime that next evening, hoping that Mom would breastfeed. "You feed her, " she told the nurse. I don't produce milk. I didn't breastfeed any of my kids." The nurse told Mom she'd be happy to prepare some formula, but wouldn't she want to hold and feed her daughter and welcome her to the world?

Mom said she told the nurse to go away. "I'm tired, and I need my rest."

IN THE BEGINNING ...

The first time my mom shared the story of my birth, I was eager for some positive insights about my arrival into the world—the joy I brought to my parents, their anticipation, and their love. By the time she finished, I felt crushed and humiliated. Mom detailed her rejection of me, her disgust, and her regret over my existence to everyone in the room. When I got older, I questioned her about my birth story, desperate to understand why she rejected me. Her response was devastating. "You had all that shit on you. It was disgusting. I couldn't stand to look at you, let alone touch you." After that, I learned not to ask.

As I embarked upon my healing journey, I revisited this painful story. It was through this reflection that I grasped the deep-seated impact of origin stories. Origin stories tell us who we are and how we came to be, serving as the foundation upon which we build our lives. Everyone has a narrative about their beginnings. My mother's initial feelings of disgust and rejection were deeply ingrained in me. A strong, positive origin story instills a sense of security and connection. While a happy origin story doesn't guarantee success, it can foster crucial self-awareness as we navigate adulthood.

WHEN IT COMES TO ORIGIN STORIES, THERE ARE SEVERAL KEY FACTORS TO CONSIDER:

Family Dynamics: Understanding origin stories within the context of our families is essential. On the day we're born, we're like actors stepping into the spotlight, diving into an ongoing story. Unlike actors, we have no clue where we are, who the other characters are, their backstories, or what our role is. We haven't had any rehearsals or preparation or a script or director to guide us.

Effects on an Infant's Emerging Awareness: Through my years of experience, training, therapy, and working with clients, I've learned that infants and children are essentially forced to improvise until they establish a sense of self, crafting a character for the role they'll play in their own story while navigating their family's preexisting narrative. But how exactly do infants and children construct their story and, consequently, their identity? Exploring the elements of storytelling provides a captivating insight into human development.

Infant babies aren't just passive lumps; they're incredibly curious and absorbent learners right from the start. During infancy, the brain undergoes rapid growth, with new neural connections forming quickly, laying the groundwork for future learning and development. Babies gather information by engaging all their senses—they see, hear, touch, taste, and smell the world around them, each encounter adding to the narrative they're writing. They also keenly observe the behaviors and actions of those around them, integrating what they see and experience into their own evolving stories.

Mimicking Behavior: As adults, we often do things without fully understanding why. Sometimes, it's endearing, like when I look at old photos of my stepson sitting next to his dad, mirroring his every move, from their arm placement to how they cross their legs. On the flip side, mirroring family behaviors can sometimes lead to negative outcomes. Take, for example, a client who couldn't figure out why she always needed to put on makeup before making coffee. It wasn't until we talked that she recalled observing her mother doing the same thing when she was a baby and being taught to do so when she started experimenting with makeup. Similarly, seeing my parents smoke cigarettes normalized the behavior for me, so when I reached high school, I dove right into experimentation. It's not to blame my parents; rather, after years of observation and endless exposure to cigarette ads—especially prevalent in the 1960s and 1970s—it became a familiar and accepted behavior. And a part of my story.

Generational Messages: Every family carries a deep history that shapes the identities of its members. From parents to grandparents and beyond, we inherit more than just traditions—we absorb generational stories that shape how we see ourselves and the world around us. In my family, for instance, I grew up with the knowledge that my parents were first-generation Americans. Their immigrant backgrounds instilled in them a relentless work ethic, along with deep-rooted beliefs about the hardships and struggles of life.

Both sides of my family had unique journeys. My maternal grandparents fled the Balkan Wars in the early 1900s, while my father's family left Italy for a better life in America in the late 1800s. With them, they carried cultural beliefs about gender roles, the kind of work they valued, and how families should be structured. Religion played a significant role as well, creating tension between my mother's Russian Orthodox faith and my father's Roman Catholic upbringing.

These stories of past generations become the legacies we unknowingly carry forward. They shape our beliefs, our decisions, and how we navigate the world.

Social Interactions and Emotions: Babies actively process everything they encounter, using this information to connect with their surroundings. They start identifying patterns in their environment and learn to anticipate what comes next, aiding their understanding of the world. Through exploration, babies begin grasping the concept of actions and consequences, a crucial step in their learning and problem-solving journey. Additionally, infants are highly sensitive to the emotions of those around them. They can distinguish between happy and sad faces and respond accordingly.

Mom's emotions were in turmoil following my arrival. She grappled with depression, exacerbated by hormonal shifts and the challenges of a troubled marriage, compounded by the onset of more severe mental health issues. Changing my diapers was a particular struggle for her. In the 1950s, women used cloth diapers that needed washing or sending out to a laundry service. Our old washer with ringers made the process arduous, especially with the volume of diapers generated by a newborn. With Mom exhausted and managing a baby and two other kids, and a husband offering no help, she opted not to change my diapers as frequently. There were times when I'd sit in a soiled diaper for days. Instead of enduring the discomfort, I learned to control my bathroom urges. To this day, I possess an incredible ability to hold my pee when needed. However, the downside is that I've battled constipation throughout my life.

Belonging: Children also possess an innate need for belonging. The family serves as their first encounter with belonging, and depending on how this experience unfolds, it can profoundly shape their personal narrative. Belonging fosters feelings of security, support, and self-worth. As the primary social group, family plays a pivotal role in teaching children about relationships, trust, and the concept of "home," which embodies love and acceptance. From this foundation, children broaden their sense of belonging through healthy relationships and a strong sense of self. Upon examination, we often uncover core beliefs about ourselves and the world that stem from our origin stories.

THE IMPACT OF MY ORIGIN STORY

Because I experienced rejection starting from the day I was born, my origin story—and consequently, my life story—was characterized by distrust, self-loathing, and an intense longing to belong, to blend in. This longing was so far-reaching that I became a chameleon, adapting myself to fulfill my deep-seated need for connection. With my family, I instinctively understood that my survival depended on fitting in. I had to mold myself into someone my mom and dad would approve of. This became a significant aspect of my origin story and a deeply ingrained behavior that influenced my life for decades.

It wasn't until years later that I discovered a system that resonated with me and propelled my healing progress to new heights. One of my mentors recommended delving into IBP – Integrative Body Psychotherapy. IBP's focus was on unraveling the family dynamics during infancy. Developed by Jack Rosenberg and Beverly Kitaen-Morse, IBP offered a yearlong program centered on how emotions from early childhood become lodged in the body. Through breathing and movement exercises, I learned how to navigate through these emotions. What particularly captivated me was the concept of the Primary Scenario. The Primary Scenario is a map of your childhood family, where each family and extended family member becomes a potential character. As I worked with this map, I realized its crucial role in the origin story process. It provided a snapshot of my family's life on the day I was born.

My journey with IBP, which involved uncovering the underlying beliefs and systems shaping subconscious and unconscious perceptions, proved invaluable in reshaping my narrative by dissecting my family's dynamics and empowering me to make new choices.

THE PLOT THICKENS: MY FAMILY'S STORY

Dad never wanted to marry, but when Mom got pregnant with my older sister, Sally, after unsuccessfully trying to get Dad to propose, things changed. Dad was handsome and loved the ladies and gambling. Mom, an Eastern European beauty, met Dad, and sparks flew. At age 28—which was considered old for a single woman in the 1950s—she decided Dad was "the one." Mom came from a large family in rural Pennsylvania. Her parents had met on a boat from Serbia, fleeing the turmoil of the Balkan Wars. While I never met Mom's dad, her mother, my Baba, never learned to read or write English and could barely speak it.

Observing her sisters, I know it had to be tough for Mom. They were cruel, often criticizing her:

"James is a lazy gambler!"

"You could have done so much better!"

"Why did you wait so long? All the great guys you could have married. And then you marry that Italian?"

They always pronounced "Italian" with a long "I" as in "Eye-talian." I shudder to think what they must have called her when she was single in her late twenties. When I was a teenager, Mom constantly hounded me about getting married because I needed someone to take care of me. She thought marriage was my destiny, mirroring the path her family had in mind for her.

When Mom and Dad met, she was managing the candy department at an A&P Grocery store in Pittsburgh. Dad drove a truck for A&P part-time and occasionally stopped by the store where she worked. He immediately pursued her. Mom was tall, with high cheekbones and a beautiful smile. Dad looked like the actor Robert Taylor. Like Mom, he was a first-generation American. Their temperaments were volatile, and their passions were intense. There was as much fighting and breaking up as there was making up.

Mom knew she had to marry to get her family off her back. As the fourth of six girls, her three older sisters were already married with children. The pressure was on. She feared ending up like her younger sister, who worked as a secretary and had to find a career. With only an eighth-grade education but plenty of street smarts, Mom was determined to marry Dad. When crying, cajoling, threats, and ultimatums failed, she stopped using her diaphragm and became pregnant. Growing up in the era of happy 1950s TV families like *Leave it to Beaver* and *Father Knows Best*, I was immersed in the idea of perfect family dynamics. In these shows, wives stayed home while husbands worked, and girls had nicknames like "Kitten" and "Princess." Married couples slept in separate beds, avoiding any implication of sex. Mom tried to drill it into our heads that sex before marriage was only for "bad girls," while boys, having "needs," were allowed to sleep with someone, though that poor girl would be labeled a slut.

There was a lot of shame around our sexuality, but I didn't understand the even greater depth of Mom's shame for "having" to marry. Her family never let her forget it. They chided her about her anniversary date and asked why she didn't have proper wedding photos while proudly displaying their own. I watched Mom droop whenever the harassment started, never understanding why her sisters treated her so poorly. As a child observing this behavior, I absorbed all the hurt, pain, and fear around me without explanation, thinking that was just how life worked. It wasn't until my early teens that I discovered Mom's first pregnancy was the reason for their conduct.

After Mom and Dad married, Sally arrived, and Dad was smitten. His heart opened in ways he couldn't imagine. I later learned Dad was more loving than he let on, adoring his mother, Grandma Carrie, who was everything to him. Dad hated his father, Frank, for having affairs and living part-time with a "Side Piece." Grandma Carrie, a devout Roman Catholic, would never divorce and tried to accept Frank's other women, but Dad saw her hurt and never forgave him. Dad swore he'd never marry and do to someone what his father had done to his beloved mother. Sally changed his views on marriage. Dad embraced family life and aimed to be a different man. Mom was thrilled, and when she became pregnant again, delivering a boy, Dad was over the moon. His family was complete. He took a full-time job driving trucks with A&P, gave up gambling, and bought a three-bedroom house. Life was perfect. And then it wasn't.

Just after they moved into their new home, Grandma Carrie died. Dad was devastated. He was with her in the hospital when she died, while Grandpa Frank was out with the Side Piece. Dad withdrew. Mom hated that Dad loved his mother more than her and tried everything to get him back, reminding him of his happiness with family through scheduled home photo sessions and home decoration. Nothing worked. She stopped using her diaphragm again and got pregnant with me, hoping my birth would win him back. When she announced her pregnancy, Dad was angry and, as I mentioned earlier, told her to get rid of the baby. But Mom was determined. She named me after his mother, either out of spite or hope. It didn't work. Dad didn't want anything to do with me, and when Mom realized her plan failed, she didn't want me either.

When I entered the family, I didn't know any of these dynamics. I only wanted food, a clean diaper, and affection.

Around the time I was two, Mom tried again to win back Dad and had another child. She thought a son would do the trick and listed names for her new son. When my younger sister arrived, Mom named her after Dad's sister, Tessa, hoping it would work. It didn't. By then, Dad was completely withdrawn, gambling again, and eventually, he left his full-time job. Money was scarce. We lived on whatever income came from odd jobs. I remember Mom keeping a yellow-lined notepad listing all the bills and how much she could pay for each. Meals consisted of pasta and iceberg lettuce. At night, I heard my parents' whispered conversations about bills and the mortgage.

Plot Points

To Recap:

- Understanding your familial structures and the stories that developed from them can give you valuable insights into your origin story.
- The family is the first social group we encounter. The dynamics within this group, including parents and parental figures, siblings, and extended family, play a crucial role in shaping our sense of self, our beliefs about the world, and how we interact with others.
- Family experiences, both positive and negative, become building blocks of our origin stories. These experiences shape our values, resilience, and how we cope. The stories we hear about our family history, triumphs, and struggles become part of our own narrative. These stories influence our sense of identity and belonging.
- Family stories reveal patterns that repeat across generations. By understanding these patterns, you can elect to break the cycle and create a different future for yourself. Also, family secrets and unhealed emotional wounds can have a lasting impact on future generations. Acknowledging and processing these issues can be a powerful step towards healing.
- Family stories can also highlight the resilience and strength shown by family members in challenging times. These stories can inspire your own journey.

Examples of Family Stories

Immigration: My parents were first-generation Americans raised in families with distinct cultural customs and distinctions. Their upbringing influenced their religious practices, acceptable behavior patterns, and gender roles in addition to several other traditions and rules. By examining these, I discovered certain conditions I adopted—and then excluded—from my story.

Generational Trauma: Surviving wars, national disasters, and racism are just a few types of generational trauma. Understanding the role of this story is important in working with your origin story.

Nepotism: If your relatives are wealthy or influential, particularly celebrities and politicians, you've probably heard the term "Nepo Baby." How has your family's social status affected your worldview?

These are just three examples of family stories that can affect your personal origin story. As you move through the steps below, you can unravel the impact of your forebears' stories and empower your own.

What's Your Story?

To discover your origin story, follow these steps:

Step 1: Create a Family Tree

Start with your birth family. Ask these questions:

- Are you an only child?
- Where are you in the birth order?
- Describe your parents' families. Were they only children? Adopted?
- Review your parents' family tree, including grandparents, aunts, and uncles, and see how it aligns with yours.
- Talk to family members and ask about the stories they heard growing up.

Exploring your ancestry can be enriching. Various websites and services offer access to historical records, photos, and family details. For example, when I researched my family, I found photos of my grandparents I'd never seen, revealing a strong family resemblance and more about their history. This gave me a new and valuable sense of myself.

If you were adopted, describe your adoptive family and anything you know about your birth family.

Record the feelings that arise during this exercise.

Step 2: Examine Relationships

Look at the relationships in your family.

- What adjectives were used to describe your family members? Were they controlling, supportive, loving, or non-present?
- What was your relationship with your parents and siblings like?

- Consider your parents' nationalities and how this aspect may (or may not) have impacted your origin story.
- Did you feel safe and comfortable? What challenges did you notice in your family as you were growing up?

Step 3: Write About Your Family Influence

Document your findings:

- How did your extended family influence you?
- Were you close with your family? Was it an easy closeness?
- How did your family treat you, and how did you treat them?
- Describe relationships with your immediate family members, as well as your grandparents, aunts, and uncles.

Step 4: Note Significant Events

Identify important events in your life. How did they affect you? Consider events like the birth of a sibling, the loss of a parent or family member, or a divorce.

Step 5: Analyze Patterns

Review everything you've gathered. Do you see any patterns in your life today that link back to your family?

For example, in my life, I struggled to form friendships with women. Repeatedly, I tried to befriend women who ultimately rejected me. Recognizing this pattern, I realized I was recreating the original rejection from my mom and older sister. With these insights, connect your family's beginnings with your current life.

Complete the following chart assessing the following areas of your life:

- Repeated Patterns
- Thoughts about Life, Happiness, and Abundance

- Love, Relationships, and Friends
- Career and Lifestyle

Identify specific behaviors or beliefs and note their origins. Then, take a moment to reflect and explain each area. Use the chart below to help you in this process. You can find downloadable PDF copies of the chart and more on my website at carriekcwest.com.

(In this chart, I've used examples from my life.)

Area	**Behavior or Belief**	**Origin**	**Explanation**
Repeated Patterns	Fear of outdoor sports	Mom was overprotective	Mom's brother suffered a severe injury playing football in high school, which led him to become depressed and isolated.
Thoughts about Life, Happiness, Abundance	Other people's happiness comes before mine.	Rejected by my parents, I felt lost and unworthy.	Because I was rejected, I believed that if I could prove my worth to my family, they would finally accept me.
Love, Relationships, and Friends	Just get married already!	I received powerful messages from my parents and society about my role in life.	Growing up in the 1960s, I was told to find a guy and get married, regardless of whether I loved him or not.
Career and Lifestyle	You don't need a career; you need a husband	My parents and extended family discouraged me from following my dreams, pushing me toward marriage instead.	My parents, coming from immigrant families, believed a woman's role was to stay at home and have children.

This chart is a powerful tool for boosting self-awareness and reshaping your narrative whenever needed.

3

Story Arc

How many times do I have to teach you: just because something works doesn't mean it can't be improved.

— Shuri, *Black Panther*

May 1958

Whenever Mom told this story, she always started it with, "It was such a beautiful day."

It was May 1958. She was eight months pregnant and miserable as she sat in her familiar, comfy spot on the sofa, next to the end table with her coffee and cigarettes. Mom was alone that morning in the living room, cluttered with the previous night's movie-time wreckage. She had no desire or energy to do anything about the mess.

"I'm so tired," she said out loud before sinking back into the sofa. She lit a cigarette and took a sip of her coffee. Neither calmed her as she had hoped. She started to close her eyes when she noticed movement from the left hallway. There I stood. Nineteen months old, damp diaper limp around my otherwise naked self. Mom said that I scrambled down the hallway on my wobbly legs. She smiled. No matter how much she hated being a mother to her three-almost-four children, she said that I was the one who surprised her. Mom said my determination was apparent even then. And since I had stopped using the crib and now slept in a bed, keeping me in my room and out of the way was difficult.

Mom said I hobbled around the room, a huge smile on my face, ready to see what the day held. My new front teeth, two on top, two on bottom, showed; my tiny frame was small for a baby my age.

Mom relayed that she wondered about feeding me but was too tired to move. She thought I could wait a while. In the meantime, I continued exploring the mess around the room. On the coffee table rested a large white plastic bowl. Inside was the leftover popcorn from movie night.

Mom said she watched me as I reached into the bowl and found the leftover popcorn. I stuck my tiny hand in and grabbed a handful. I put the popcorn in my mouth, held my hand there, and gummed the tasty morsels. I swallowed, grabbed some more, and, once again, put them in my mouth. I repeated this a few more times until I was full. A look of peace came across my face. After so much time, I was finally satisfied.

Mom watched as I scurried back down the hallway. I went to my room, crawled into bed, and slept while Mom closed her eyes and let her own sleep take hold.

Later that day, after Mom had prepared dinner, she thought about me and realized she hadn't seen or heard me all day. Mom dragged her heavy body into my room and found me fast asleep. "James must have fed her. About time he did something around here." She rambled back to the living room and the evening television. The next morning, after her older two children were off to school, she checked on her youngest and found me still asleep. She noticed a wet diaper and nothing smelly, so she let me sleep. A couple of hours later Mom checked again. This time, my eyes were open, and my tummy was swollen and firm to the touch. Mom lifted me and found me listless but not fevered, so she laid me back in bed to rest. The next morning, Mom heard crying. She slumbered out of bed and into my room. My belly was fully distended, and I was warm. Mom put me down, left the room, and shut the door behind her. She stood for a moment outside the door wondering. Then she went on her way, thinking, "She can cry herself to sleep."

Just before lunch, the doorbell rang. Mom opened the door and found her pediatrician, Dr. Saul, standing there. "I was in the neighborhood and thought I'd check on everyone. Can I come in?" Mom later wondered what force called the doctor to her door that very moment on that very day. She knew he made house calls, but she did not recall him dropping in like this. She let him in and said, "My youngest has been crying all morning. Her stomach is sticking out. Perhaps you can look."

Panicked, he said, "Take me to her now!" Mom brought him to my room. He took one look at me and yelled, "What have you fed her?" Mom told him about the popcorn.

"Grab me some towels and get some hot water. Go!" Mom left the room to do as he demanded. The doctor opened his bag and grabbed his rubber gloves, ointment, and a syringe. Mom came back with the towels and water. The doctor went to work removing the undigested popcorn from my blocked digestive system. Mom said I screamed as the doctor worked.

Afterward, he cleaned me as I sucked my thumb, my face wet with tears. Mom saw that I was breathing and looked like a wreck from the ordeal. An hour or so more, and I would have died from the rotting food in my system. The doctor brought the soiled items to Mom. She vomited at the smell and told the doctor to throw everything away.

The next day and for many weeks after, Dr. Saul made regular visits to see me. He brought proper food and made sure I ate until I was full. He'd suspected something was amiss and was glad he had trusted his instincts to stop by.

◇◇

THE ARC OF A PERSONAL STORY

In what I've come to call My Popcorn Story, my days as a toddler were filled with exploration and discovery. I remember zooming around the house, outside, or wherever I was, enjoying the freedom my tiny legs gave me. At that point, I had no idea that my Mom's lack of care was not a usual way of life. It was my experience of life.

When life is viewed as a story, it's important to include the concept of a story arc. The story arc in a personal narrative is the story's movement from start to finish. **My Popcorn Story** demonstrates the components of the story arc. The first is the Beginning. The story's start sets the stage, introducing me coming down the hall to see what's going on in the living room.

The next step in the story process is called the Inciting Incident. The Inciting Incident is the event that starts the journey. While it can be shocking, that's not a requirement. The key is that this event opens the door to a story that ultimately changes you and alters your life in some way. In **My Popcorn Story**, eating the popcorn set the plot of my life in motion and thrust me into the central conflict of my narrative. It was a major turning point that propelled me forward on my journey.

The main section of the story is called the Rising Action. In this section, the character navigates life, confronting challenges, making crucial decisions, or repeating mistakes, increasing the tension until the story reaches its climax. In **My Popcorn Story**, Mom checked on me a few times during the two days I was suffering but took no action, escalating the stakes in what was potentially a life-threatening event.

The Climax, or Defining Moment, is the point at which the stakes are highest. It's the "now or never" moment where something has to change. Dr. Saul's arrival was the climax of **My Popcorn Story**. If he hadn't, my life would have been over.

This leads you to The Resolution. The resolution is where the protagonist realizes something significant and undergoes a transformation. She is no longer the person she was at the story's beginning. My near brush with death terrified me. On some level, I discovered I wasn't in a safe environment and that the people I thought were my caretakers were anything but. Mom told me I became more withdrawn after that incident and only seemed relaxed when the doctor was around. I went from a smiling, curious toddler to a cautious one, sucking my thumb for self-comfort.

My Popcorn Story example is a microcosm of the arc of a story in action. In your personal story, you'll have multiple arcs that can move quickly over a few days or can last a lifetime.

Working with the arc of your personal story helps uncover themes that I'll discuss in a later chapter. Looking back on life, you can find challenges you've overcome and goals you've achieved, which can bring a sense of purpose and well-being. This also means you can see your motivations and behavioral patterns, empowering you to take control of your narrative, and even rewrite chapters and create new ones.

Quite often, personal stories aren't linear. In my exploration of stories and in working with clients, I have experienced unexpected twists and turns that, at the time, I might have thought derailed the process. The key is to see that every unexpected occurrence is simply a tiny obstacle to address and then move beyond; each is a part of the larger story arc.

THE PLOT THICKENS

Viewing personal experience through the lens of story arc offers more than just a timeline; it's a tribute to someone's resilience, growth, and lessons learned along the way. My own story is filled with examples of this, but one of my client's stories is even more compelling.

"Jill" was in an emotionally abusive marriage. Her husband was controlling and, over time, convinced her to end most of her friendships and give up her hobbies to do everything with him. He verbally attacked her and almost wiped out any self-esteem she had. She came to me after a couple of her friends tried one last time to reach her. They convinced her that her marriage was a mess. Their intervention reached a kernel of self-love that was still inside Jill. She came to me filled with doubts and defenses. The difficult step was for her to realize that her current situation was not how marriage worked. It was from this starting point that we created a story arc.

She determined the inciting incident to be her wedding day. Before the wedding, her husband was a loving and supportive partner. They socialized with other couples and pursued both individual and shared interests. However, after the wedding, things gradually changed. By their second anniversary, Jill had become a completely different person.

To understand the rising actions, I asked Jill to document the obstacles that began after the wedding. Initially, her husband would joke about how much time she spent with her friends, leaving him to fend for himself. He talked about a partnership that meant doing everything together. Jill tried to make him feel less alone, which only increased his manipulations. Her husband was persistent and eventually Jill decided it was easier to go along with what he wanted. However, this only worsened the situation. He became angry at even the slightest mistakes, criticizing her cooking, the items she bought at the market, her clothes, her hair, and how she seemed to be stooped over much of the time.

I was heartbroken as she shared the challenges she faced in her five years of marriage, but I congratulated her on her courage to confront her experience head-on. She had reached a decision point: was she ready to write a new chapter? Due to the psychological toll her marriage had taken, I advised her to engage a therapist to work through the emotions and damage. To her credit, she did, and after six months, she had the strength to move out. Her husband wasn't happy and tried to win her back for some time. Jill filed for divorce and moved to a different state. Once settled in her new home, she restarted our work together, and with my help, wrote a new chapter in her life.

Plot Points

To Recap:

- Story arcs start with an inciting incident that disrupts your life and sets you on a path of change as in the above story, Jill's wedding.
- Rising action includes obstacles—internal struggles, external conflicts, or unexpected events—that lead to a climax. In Jill's story, her husband's manipulation began innocently enough after the wedding but gradually increased in frequency and intensity until it reached a decision point.
- Overcoming these challenges brings personal growth and development. Jill's willingness to take action and change her circumstances raised her self-esteem.
- The resolution is the culmination of your journey. With valuable lessons learned, new skills acquired, and a fresh perspective on life, you are ready for a new chapter. For Jill, this meant finding the courage to end her marriage and move on with her life as a different and fully capable woman.

What's Your Story?

Now, let's apply these concepts to your life:

Step 1: Find your inciting incident

- When looking at your life, the first and most important inciting incident was the day you were born. Everything that happens after that is the rising action that takes you on the journey of being alive. Along the way, numerous inciting incidents bring you fulfilling (and sometimes dramatic) adventures.

- For this exercise, look at a current situation you want to change. For example, you might feel unfulfilled at work and want a new challenge. It may be a relationship issue that you'd like to improve. It could also mean overall happiness.

- Choose the situation you want to address and decide to take action to achieve your goal. This decision to take action is your inciting incident. For example, I had a client who was a college professor seeking job security. When his university had tenure openings, he was passed over. Asking for help marked the beginning of his journey.

Step 2: Rising action

When writers work on a story, whether it's for film or television or even when they are writing a book, the most interesting part of the tale is the rising action. This is where the journey unfolds. The protagonist is taken through various twists and turns to reach their final goal: to be a changed person. Let's see how this is applied to your narratives:

- Looking at the inciting incident you've selected, think about the steps you'll take to reach your goal. For example, the client who wanted tenure made it a point to meet the members of the tenure committee, expressing his desire to be a permanent member of staff. He also updated them on the research he did to show that he was a valuable asset to the university. He took other steps as well, but the point is that with my help, he created a plan to reach his dream.

- In your rising action, list the steps you can take. Here are other examples:
  - — With careers, what steps can you take to improve your skills or develop new ones that inspire you? Perhaps take classes or join a mentorship program.
  - — In relationships, if you're looking to date, perhaps join a dating site or ask friends to introduce you to other people. I also recommend participating in hobbies that you enjoy where you're likely to meet people with similar interests.
  - — If you're looking for more overall happiness, you might think about volunteering or joining a local activity. One of my clients loved to cook and found a local chef that offered classes. She learned new techniques and recipes that she shared with family and friends to rave reviews.

Step 3: Resolution

This is your desired outcome, your dream fulfilled.

- The first step in your personal narrative is to know the resolution you want. Writing it in your journal is a great way to give it substance.
- Hopefully you've listed steps to take in your journal to reach your goal. Note the ones completed and include a thought on how you'll know you've reached it. Here are some ideas:

— In relationships, you've started dating someone or you've made a new friend as a result of the steps taken.

— With your career, you may have received a long-overdue promotion or were acknowledged by your peers for something you achieved.

— In your life, you realize one day that you are feeling calmer and more relaxed and generally happier.

- Make a note of the success in your notebook and celebrate it! YOU DID IT!

Step 4: Final Thoughts:

At times throughout this process, obstacles can arise. View these challenges as guideposts to a possible need for a course correction. For example, if a person at work is constantly frustrating you, you don't need to change jobs to have a resolution. Sometimes, the quest is to respond differently to the person while maintaining a level of calm and happiness within yourself.

- Each step you take is a vital part of the story arc and, when viewed as such, can lighten the experience.

- Incorporating the concept of a story arc into your personal story gives you a powerful tool for navigating life's journey with purpose and empowerment.

4

Heroes and Villains

> In the movies, we have leading ladies, and we have the best friend. You, I can tell, are a leading lady. But for some reason, you're behaving like the best friend.
>
> — Arthur, *The Holiday*

September 1962

The house was chaotic. My sister, Sally, scrambled to get ready for the first day of school. Sally wanted to get out the door before Mom forced her to walk with me to my first day of school. Unfortunately, Dad wasn't home that morning to intervene on her behalf, so she knew she'd have to do it. Sally hated me, always had. Sally was okay with our brother but never understood why Mom and Dad wanted me or our younger sister. She wanted nothing to do with us.

"Sally!" Mom's scream shook her out of her reverie.

"What? I'm right here!" Sally said. Mom came into the living room. It was in its usual messy state. Glasses—some containing water from melted ice—and bowls with crumbs in them, sat on the coffee table. Shoes were scattered around. Mom's morning coffee waited for her on the table next to the sofa, a burned-out cigarette in the full ashtray. The room smelled of old food and cigarettes. Sally was dressed in her new school dress and shoes. She stood with her arms folded. Mom walked into the room pulling me by the arm behind her. I scrambled to keep up. I wore a dress that was

Sally's once upon a time, and new shoes that were just a little too big. Mom handed me to Sally and said, "Make sure she gets to her classroom. She's in first grade so someone in the office will know where she's supposed to go."

Sally looked aghast. "Why can't you take her? My friends are waiting for me. She's too slow."

Mom was not in the mood. "Because I said so. You have to take care of your sister. I'm busy." Mom glared at her oldest child, wishing her out of her sight. "Just go. You'll be late. Hold her hand!"

Sally grabbed my arm and dragged me with her out the door and to a street already cluttered with neighborhood kids on their way to school. Sally held my arm until we were far enough away that mom couldn't see us. She saw her friends ahead and rushed to catch up with them. I tried to keep up, moving as fast as I could, terrified I'd be left behind. My feet started to hurt from the blisters forming from my new shoes. But I knew it was dangerous to stop. We eventually made it to the bottom of the hill where William Penn Elementary School was starting to fill with students for the new school year. A crossing guard waited at the side to make sure the kids crossed the street safely. I caught up to Sally who reluctantly took my arm. She knew the teachers would report her to Mom if I showed up on my own. We walked up the hill together, Sally excited to be among her friends; me terrified, not knowing a thing about where I was going and why. The closer we got to the building, the more strangers I saw, the more terrified I became. After what seemed like forever, we finally reached the front door. I stopped before the steps to enter. I tried to speak, "Sally." It was almost a whisper. But Sally ignored me and pulled away.

"Sally." This time louder. Sally stopped.

"What?" she said sharply.

I replied, "I'm scared."

"Oh, too bad. Just go into your room." Sally walked inside the building and left me standing there while all the other kids, their parents and teachers rushed around me to their classes. I started to

cry. I knew crying was wrong, so I put my thumb in my mouth and stood frozen to the spot trying hard to hold back the tears falling down my face. After what felt like an eternity, a young woman came and bent down to face me.

"Are you lost?" The kindness in her voice pushed me over the edge. I burst into tears and cried out. The woman grabbed a tissue from her pocket and dried my tears. She took another tissue and helped me blow my nose before taking me to the school office. "Can you tell me your name? If you do, I can help you find your room."

Thumb firmly planted in my mouth, I said, "I want Sally."

The woman looked at me. "Who is Sally."

I removed my thumb. "My sister. She's here."

The woman looked at the others in the office. "What's your name?"

"Carrie."

"What's your last name?"

I hesitated a moment hoping I wasn't in trouble. "Powell."

The woman looked at a chart. "Sally Powell. Sixth grade. I'll go get her."

As I sat in the chair, more tears started to fill my eyes. I looked at my feet and saw the traces of blood on my white socks from the blisters on my feet. Mom would not like that. Soon, Sally walked into the office. I saw my sister and burst into tears again.

Sally was not amused. "Would you stop embarrassing me?" She turned to the woman in the office. "She's my sister. Starting first grade. Can I go now?"

I said, "You didn't say goodbye. You just left me."

Sally rolled her eyes. "Okay… goodbye, you little creep. Can I go now?" The woman who found me nodded and Sally left. After a few minutes, she took my hand and walked me to my class. She noticed the blood on my socks and asked me if I needed a Band-Aid. I shook my head "no." The young woman nodded. She looked sad when she said goodbye at the door.

CHARACTERS: THE HEART OF OUR STORIES

My sister, Sally, was one of the main characters in my life story. For the most part, she ignored me, but at crucial times, she would drop into the story and create havoc, undermining some of my most cherished endeavors.

Characters are the essence of any story. They drive the plot, support themes, and evoke emotions and motivations in the protagonist. Without characters, there's no story, no arc, and no resolution.

In life stories, characters aren't just the people around you; they include inner voices that play significant roles. Naming these inner characters adds depth to your narrative. For instance, I had a Critic and a Judge constantly commenting on my actions. I worked hard to dismantle them. My inner Objector warned me against risky decisions, so I sent it on a long-needed vacation. My Dreamer, who encourages me to follow my heart, now has a starring role in my story. Both internal and external characters shape your experiences, teach you lessons, and define your relationships.

In any story, the protagonist is the central character. As the author of your life story, you are the star. However, unresolved issues can shift the focus to others, such as a family member you're trying to please. For instance, I focused on gaining my father's love in many of my stories. His lack of approval overshadowed my achievements, turning him into the protagonist of my story. Instead of making my story about me, I centered it around my dad.

Consider another example from a client, Kim. After her son grew up, her marriage lost its spark. When an exciting career opportunity arose, her husband wanted her to stay home, but Kim chose to follow her passion, remaining the star of her story. This decision led to a successful career and eventually a divorce. Kim took responsibility for her life, refused to let her husband dictate her narrative, and now lives her dream.

Here are some examples of typical characters in our life journeys:

- The antagonist opposes the protagonist. This opposition pushes the story forward. In fiction, the antagonist is clear, but in real life, it could be anyone or anything that challenges your happiness and fulfillment. For me, my mother was often the antagonist, preparing me to take care of her rather than pursuing my life purpose.
- There's the Sage, who provides wisdom and mentorship.
- Other characters include the Love Interest, the Comic Relief, the Best Friend and the Foil. Sally, my sister was my Foil. She made my life difficult, as seen in the opening story about walking to school and in this next example from junior high, when becoming a cheerleader was my ultimate dream.

I practiced tirelessly for the cheerleading team, perfecting my cheers, flips, and somersaults. One of the faculty cheer sponsors noticed my efforts and helped me with my handstands, boosting my confidence. I made it to the final tryouts, and with only six of us competing for four spots, I felt ready.

On the day of the tryouts, excitement outweighed my nerves. I watched the other girls and then gave my best performance, nailing every handstand, flip, and split. The judges smiled, and I was sure I had made it. That night, I shared my excitement with my family. Mom commented on transportation, Dad grumbled, and Sally gave me a look. My younger sister Tessa, however, gave me a cheerleader charm for my bracelet, which I took as a sign that things were looking up.

The results were posted that Friday. I rushed to the gymnasium, my heart pounding. But my name wasn't on the list. I checked again and again, disbelief turning to heartbreak. They had chosen Connie Blocker, a tiny girl who didn't even know the routines. I was devastated.

I approached the sponsor who had helped me, seeking answers. Her response cut deep: "Carrie, you were great! But Sally called and mentioned your struggles adjusting to the new school. We thought it might be too much for you, so we gave the spot to Connie. It seemed like the best decision."

At dinner that night, I confronted Sally. "Why? You're going to college. What does it matter to you?"

She smiled and simply said, "Because I could." My heart shattered. This is classic Foil behavior.

Recognizing the characters in your life story helps you understand your experiences and relationships. This awareness enables you to rewrite your narrative, placing yourself as the protagonist and making empowered choices.

THE PLOT THICKENS

Have you ever watched a show where they switch characters or recast actors? James Bond movies are famous for this, using different actors to keep the franchise alive. It also happens in films like *Iron Man*, *Harry Potter*, and *The Dark Knight*. The character's role stays the same even if the actor changes. James Bond is always the hero, Professor Dumbledore remains The Sage, and Colonel Rhodes stays The Close Friend.

The same pattern plays out in our personal stories. When I was dating, I constantly fell for guys who weren't interested in me, mirroring my relationship with my father. This pattern repeated with female friends, as well. In my thirties, I joined a women's group that met monthly. It was a valuable opportunity to connect and share ideas.

After one meeting, I invited Colleen, a smart and articulate woman, to lunch. She seemed interested, but after ignoring my email and text, she politely declined, citing her busy schedule.

Months later, I tried again, expressing my hope for friendship. She reiterated that she was too busy but might find time later.

Feeling humiliated and rejected, I continued with the group but became less engaged. Over time, members came and went. Three years later, during a therapy session, I realized I had cast Colleen in the "mom" role in my Life Story. Her rejection had reopened old wounds from my mother. Like actors who get typecast, we continue playing the same roles in our own lives – like actor Hugh Grant playing the leading man in romantic comedies or Joe Pesci as a gangster. I kept playing the role of seeking connection with people who weren't interested, leaving me feeling rejected and unworthy, continuously reliving the patterns of my childhood.

In our own stories, we assign roles to the people around us. To change our story, we need to rewrite the script, creating compelling, well-suited characters who support our dream ending.

Plot Points

To Recap:

- Knowing the characters of your life and their relationships to your story is crucial to changing the plot.
- We might not be the star of every story we are telling. Discovering who the star is offers insights to the story we tell and how it can be changed.
- Many characters affect our story. Some are more prominent than others, but all play a role.
- We often replay the role we learned to play in our family's story.

What's Your Story?

When working with your characters, I recommend creating a chart listing the key characters in the story you're rewriting. The chart below is one I use in my work. List their names, and in the first column, note how they made you feel. In the next column, write how you related to them/who they reminded you of. This will give you an idea of your antagonist and various characters' other roles. You'll see how you recast familiar roles by recognizing who they reminded you of. Note the role they play in the last column of your chart. Use the list of Archetypes at the end of this chapter to give you ideas. You can find downloadable PDF copies of the chart and more on my website at carriekcwest.com.

(I used my experiences as examples in the chart below.)

Family Members or Other Important characters	**How They Made Me Feel**	**How I Related to Them/Who They Reminded Me Of**	**Role**
Mom	Rejected	Why did she have me?/ Same	Antagonist
Sally	Ashamed	I don't know why she hated me/Same	Foil
Internal: Objector	Doubtful	No self-trust/Mom	Antagonist
Ex-Boyfriend	Unlovable	Bad relationship/Dad	Outlaw

Step 1: Build your chart(s)

- Create a chart for each story you're working with –your Life Story (for overall happiness and fulfillment), your Relationship Story, your Career Story, your Health Story, or any others you feel are relevant.
- The characters don't need to be elaborately described, but their impact on your life story should be clear.
- Not everyone you've encountered deserves a role in your story. Focus on those who significantly impacted your journey.

Step 2: Compare charts for patterns

- Once you have the chart, review it to see if the characters' roles shift in different stories. In my college story, Dad was the star, and I was the child looking for love.
- Notice if any of the characters in your current stories play the same role originally created by someone else. For example, Colleen played my mom in my relationship story.
- List any repeat characters and their role in your current life. In my story, Sally reprised her role as Foil, which she created during my first day of school, and again with my cheerleader story.
- Examine whether you're being typecast in a role you've played repeatedly. In my case, I often found myself seeking friendships within established groups, which ultimately distracted me from the group's main purpose.
- Note what you discover in your journal.

Step 3: Reflect on what you've discovered

- Consider how your feelings towards the characters in your stories might have changed over time. For example, when I looked deeply at my relationship with Sally, I realized that she had a difficult relationship with Mom, too. I remembered a family story of Mom chasing Sally with a clothes hanger after Sally did something wrong. When I came along, Mom tried to force me on Sally. I saw a different picture of who my sister was and why she didn't care for me. With this awareness, I started developing close friendships with women, something I'd always wanted.

Step 4: Imagine your story as a movie

- Another way to look at this is to play the game I call "Who Would Play You in the Movie of Your Life?"

- Think about being at a casting call where actors are auditioning for important roles in the movie of your life. Are you casting an A-list celebrity or an unknown character actor for the starring role? What qualities of the actor made them the best choice to play you?

- What other actors do you cast in crucial roles? Who plays your mom/dad/siblings or significant other? Did you cast an actor you know who plays the villain? This exercise can be eye-opening if you approach it like a game. The goal is to reach awareness of the key characters in your story.

- Note any thoughts or insights you have in your journal. Pay attention to who these actors remind you of in your life. For instance, many people said my dad resembled the actor Robert Taylor. One day, I watched an old black-and-white movie starring Robert Taylor, where he played a debonair swashbuckling hero. As I watched, I thought, "Yep. That's exactly how I see my dad."

CHARACTER ARCHETYPES

Another technique for understanding characters is to look at the archetypes associated with different roles. They are:

The Lover:	This character is guided by the heart
The Hero/Heroine:	Any character that steps up when challenged and saves the day
The Magician:	A powerful character that bends the laws of the universe to achieve their goals. In our personal stories, the magician is often the character that appears to have life always going his (or her) way
The Outlaw:	The rebel, the black sheep that doesn't follow any rules
The Explorer:	A character who is never content, always looking for the next adventure
The Sage:	A character filled with wisdom and the ability to bring new insights into any situation
The Innocent:	An untried character who believes only the best of all things
The Creator:	The visionary compelled to build the world or situation as they desire
The Ruler:	A character that takes the lead and is in charge of the situation
The Caregiver:	An honorable and loyal character who supports others
The Everyman:	A relatable character, recognizable and comfortable
The Jester:	A funny character who uses humor to speak the truth and bring comic relief

5

Theme and Motivation

> Be bold and mighty forces will come to your aid.
>
> — Elaine Miller, *Almost Famous*

February 1964

Mom was Russian Orthodox. Since there wasn't a Russian Orthodox Church near our home in Verona, Pennsylvania, Mom attended Sunday services at the local Methodist Church. It wasn't the best option, but it was drummed into her head from her religious family that weekly church services were not optional. Mom eventually found solace in the Greek Orthodox Church in Oakmont, a short drive from home, but that was after her children were in high school.

Dad's family was Roman Catholic, although Dad never bothered with religion. Dad's mother, Grandma Carrie, insisted that he take her to Mass at least once a week. After Grandma passed away, Dad was finally free of the weekly ritual. He thought all religions were filled with scam artists who were only after your weekly tithe.

When we were younger, Mom took Tessa and me to the Methodist Church. We dressed in our Sunday finest: white dresses, white ankle socks, and patent leather shoes. Tessa and I clung to each other, not really caring about whatever they were saying, just enduring the time until we got home. We sat in the Bible reading class with other youngsters while the adults listened to sermons in the main hall.

My brother Mark and my sister Sally never seemed interested in God, and Mom never insisted they attend church, thinking their souls were already too far gone to worry about church at this point. When Sally was in high school, however, she decided to embrace Catholicism after befriending some of the girls in her class who talked passionately about church and God and Jesus. Sally demanded Tessa and I go to a Catholic Church with her so that our souls could be saved. That meant we had to have our First Communion and Confirmations in the Catholic faith. And that meant we had to attend catechism classes.

At eight years old, I was a year older than the other children in the First Communion catechism class. I wasn't much taller, but I knew I was older and was ashamed that I wasn't like the others in the class. At least Tessa was with me. We stayed close together, yet apart from the other kids, as we waited on a warm Saturday morning in April in one of the classrooms at St. Joseph's Catholic Church. The room was filled with desks and smelled of antiseptic cleaners. At the beginning of class, a priest dressed in a long black cassock entered the room along with the two nuns dressed in habits. The two women were called "Sisters." Tessa and I found it amusing that the nuns were called Sisters and thought perhaps, as blood sisters, we were chosen by God, too.

Father Michael stood in front of the class, his hands placed together in a prayer pose, a serene smile on his face. With the subtlest of nods to Sister Margaret, the nun said "Children, please settle. Father Michael is here to welcome you."

The class immediately sat still and stared at the large man in front of the room. "Thank you, Sister Margaret. Hello, children." Father Michael spoke and then waited. The entire room stared.

After a moment, Sister Margaret said, "Children, it is impolite not to respond when spoken to, especially when you are welcomed by Father Michael. Let's try it again, and this time, when Father Michael greets you, say, 'Good morning, Father Michael.'" She looked at the priest, who said, "Hello, children."

"Good morning, Father Michael," we said almost in unison.

The priest went on to talk about the importance of being Catholic and how Catholics were chosen to sit at the right hand of God. We all stared at the priest, eyes wide, as he spoke of the ruin that would come to anyone who wasn't Catholic. At that realization, Tessa turned to me and said, "What about Mom? Is she going to Hell?" Tessa was upset at the thought, but before I could quiet her, the priest heard the conversation.

"Young lady. What is your name?" The priest looked at us. Tessa was frozen in fright, so I said, "Carrie Powell, sir."

"Father," the priest said.

My face warm with shame, I repeated, "Father."

"And what were you talking about that was so important you needed to interrupt me?" I recognized that sharpness at the edge of his words and tensed. I knew I was in trouble again and just wanted to get out of there ... hopefully alive.

I took a breath and looked him in the eyes. "Tessa is afraid that our mom won't get into heaven because she isn't Catholic. Is that true?" Sister Margaret started toward me, fire in her eyes at my insolence, but Father Michael stopped her.

"Well, Carrie. I am afraid that is true. Unless your mother converts to Catholicism, her soul is in danger. Do you have anything else to share?" His last words were biting, so I shook my head, "no."

Father Michael told us that we were all on our way to securing a place in heaven with our First Holy Communion. He turned the class over to Sister Margaret and Sister Theresa and left.

Over the next weeks, as much as I hated it, Sally drove me and Tessa to our Saturday lessons. The classroom grew warmer as the weeks went by. The Sisters Margaret and Theresa were terrors. One Saturday, they went around the room asking each student about the time they were baptized and about their godparents. Some of the children said they had photos or special gifts from their christening. When they came to me and Tessa, I said, "I don't know if I was baptized. I have godparents, but there aren't any photos or presents."

I was in trouble. Again. Sister Theresa was horrified. She was all of five feet tall, but in that moment, she seemed to grow ten feet and said loud enough to scare the class, "You were born of sin! Without baptism, you are forever darkened by your sin! Next week, you and your sister must bring proof of your baptism. Otherwise, you cannot have your First Holy Communion!" When Sally picked us up at the end of the lesson, we ran to the car and told her what happened, terrified that we were in big trouble.

"You were both baptized; stop crying. I'll take care of it next week." Whatever she did, the issue of being baptized was never mentioned again.

After an interminable six weeks of lessons, it was time for our First Holy Communion, scheduled for a special ceremony at the next day's mass at St. Joseph's. The girls would wear white veiled dresses like little brides, while the boys would wear suits and ties. Before anyone could take communion, the church insisted that you go to confession to make sure there weren't any sins on your soul. Every Saturday, the confessional area at the back of the church was busy with people waiting in line and those kneeling in pews and reciting whatever penance they were given so that they'd be ready to receive communion the next day. Today was our group's First Holy Confession.

St. Joseph's Church was huge and smelled of incense, holy water, and prayer. The day was warm, adding to the momentousness of the occasion. My eyes aghast, mouth open, I looked at the giant statues of saints and the stained-glass windows. A huge cross with a bent figure of the crucified Christ on it stood several pews away at the head of the altar. I held Tessa's hand and felt her tremble. I was just hoping I didn't do anything wrong like I seemed to do every week. We followed a group of young boys and girls to the back of the church near a row of three ornate doors. We knew the priest who sat with God was behind the center door. Each confessor used the right or left door. Sister Margaret led us into the pews, where we would wait our turn.

After all the weeks and lessons that were drummed into our little bodies, we were anxious but sat as still as we could. Sister Margaret warned us about misbehaving in Church. God would be watching and would be angry if we moved about. Plus, the nun had her ruler in her sleeve to give a good rap on the knuckles of any miscreants.

One by one, Sister Margaret pointed to the children to stand ready to enter a door. I was finally called. I stood by the door on the left, which Sister Margaret said led to salvation, hands held in prayer in front of me, just like I was told. I tried hard to keep my hands steady and tried to remember what I was told. I hoped the churning in my stomach would settle soon. I looked at Tessa, who was still in the pew waiting her turn but saw Sister Margaret glaring at me. I quickly turned my gaze to the floor. The door opened and another little girl from my class walked out, shaking. The little girl was white as a ghost, making my hands tremble even more. I entered the darkened space with only the barest of light and shut the door. I knelt in front of a little window, where I learned, the priest would speak. Finally, I heard the small door slide open.

"Forgive me, Father, for I have sinned. This is my first confession." I had practiced this phrase forever and was glad I said it correctly.

The priest said, "Confess your sins."

This was the tough part. Sister Margaret had given us a list of possible sins to bring up. There were the "Dishonor thy Mother and Father," "Use the Lord's name in vain," and "Lie, steal, and misbehave" sins, but I was sure I'd done none of those and couldn't think of anything I needed to confess. After a minute, it came to me.

"I did not go to church last week." There. I had one.

The priest was not happy. His voice rose, and his breath smelled like tuna and stale cigarettes. "Young Lady!" he bellowed. "God gave the life of His only son, our Lord Jesus Christ, for you, and you can't give him one hour a week of your small life?"

Not knowing I shouldn't contradict the priest, I asked, "How was I going to get here if no one drove me? Mom doesn't come to this church."

The already righteous priest was taken apart by my questioning him. I ruined everything again. "Your mother will go to Hell for not being Catholic. Your job, young lady, is to make sure your mother brings you to church every week. You must tell her it is the only way to redeem her soul in God's eyes. You must do this. Do you understand? Otherwise, you will burn in Hell for eternity!"

Now shaken that I had upset the priest—and probably God—I said shyly, "Yes, Father." I was doomed.

"Do four Our Father's and three Hail Mary's. I absolve you of your sins. Go in peace."

The little door slid shut signaling the end of confession. I stood, opened the outer door, and walked into the bright church, feeling heavier and dirtier than I did before I entered, certain I was darkened by sin, evil and undeserving.

UNDERSTANDING THEMES IN PERSONAL STORIES

The theme of a story is its foundational message or purpose. Themes drive the protagonist and answer important questions, like whether love always wins or if good beats evil. In personal stories, themes provide insights into motivations and the reasons behind choices and decisions.

Themes are the threads that weave personal stories together, giving meaning to experiences and helping to identify patterns connecting seemingly unrelated events. By identifying themes, you better understand the reasons behind your behaviors.

For example, in the above story, religion mirrored the dynamics in my family—misbehavior resulted in severe consequences, making me feel like I was always on thin ice, even with God. Exploring this revealed my underlying fear of being so awful that I'd be destroyed. Understanding your personal theme helps uncover your uniqueness and sense of self. If it's corrupted, you have an opportunity to rewrite it in a new story.

WORKING WITH THEMES

Working with themes can lead to self-discovery. They invite you to examine your beliefs, values, and perspectives and provide a framework for understanding and processing personal experiences. Writing about my personal story was cathartic and insightful.

I titled my narrative "Poor Truck Driver's Daughter." This title crystallized the central theme of my story and forced me to acknowledge who I was. It provided clues about where to focus my attention. My mom often used this phrase to belittle my dreams, such as when I wanted to take violin lessons at six years old. This title spoke to how I imagined myself and defined my persona.

I also learned through writing my story that my theme was

that if I were to overcome my fears, I needed to survive. Despite the madness and trauma, I chose to live, determined to grow up and become my own person. To do that, I needed to escape My Family's Story.

THE IMPACT OF FAMILY STORIES

Because I chose to survive, I wove my story around existing *with* my family, not away from them. While my endgame was to break free, the complexities of our shared stories made a complete break nearly impossible. My survival theme required an antagonist to battle, and my parents fit that role perfectly.

My survival theme also made me hyperaware of everything around me. I was constantly vigilant for threats. As an infant, I learned to read the tones of my parents' voices and match them with their moods. If they were in a bad place, I stayed quiet and denied my needs. If their moods were upbeat, I knew I was safe for a while.

Crying caused my mom to react negatively, not out of concern for my needs but because it disturbed her. My dad either left the room or demanded that the noise stop. Living in constant fear, I tried not to rock the boat more than my mere existence already did. Just like in my experiences with religion, I was going through life unsupported and alone.

UNDERSTANDING MOTIVATION IN PERSONAL STORIES

Motivations drive actions, and emotions fuel those motivations, forming the core of a story's theme. In my opening story, the pattern of being alone and unsupported at home and church motivated me to excel in school. Even in elementary school, I wanted my teachers to recognize my intelligence. In third grade, I performed so well in math that Mrs. Wilson excluded me from the weekly math game because no one could beat me. She called me the Math Champion and kept me on the sidelines to give the others a chance. Feeling abandoned, I made a cardboard crown, painted it gold, and decorated it with glittery math symbols to wear while the class played. I was thrilled to be the Math Champion, but Mrs. Wilson and my classmates were not impressed.

Motivation heavily influences the aspects of your life that you can control. In acting class, when a student asks, "What's my motivation?" they're essentially asking, "Why am I saying these words? Why am I doing this?" Without understanding motivation, a character lacks depth. Emotions manifest in various ways, like the rhythm and emphasis of words, facial expressions, and gestures. It's crucial to understand your motivations when you're reshaping your story.

EXPLORING MOTIVATIONS

Motivation answers the question, "Why?" For much of my life, many of my choices were driven by fear. Fear is a powerful motivator for many people, influencing decisions related to being alone, getting fired, facing rejection or abandonment, and even dealing with failure or success. When rewriting your story, focus on transitioning your motivations from fear to excitement and enthusiasm. Excitement and enthusiasm inspire confidence, energizing you to take steps toward your goals with optimism and joy. Fear, on the other hand, often leads to hesitation and pushes you toward actions that might not align with your true self. By embracing positive motivators, you empower yourself and create a more fulfilling life experience.

THE PLOT THICKENS

Stories often have multiple themes. In my family's money story, there were many arguments about finances. My dad struggled with supporting a family of four and became overwhelmed when my younger sister and I were born. Observing his fear of financial responsibility shaped my view of money and its role in life. I accepted the theme that money would solve everything. I believed that if we had enough money, my parents might even decide they wanted me, and I could stop worrying about being sent away.

Uncovering this family dynamic revealed another recurring theme in my life: lack. Lack signifies a shortage or absence of something essential. For me, it manifested as a lack of connection, safety, and freedom from fear. However, it was easier to frame my narrative around a lack of money. This, combined with my survival theme, became the cornerstone of my story and influenced how I navigated my life and finances.

Instead of exploring my true identity and pursuing my dreams, I prioritized high-paying jobs. Instead of seeking relationships based on love and acceptance, I gravitated toward individuals who replicated the dynamics of my upbringing. Instead of breaking free from my family's influence, I internalized their story, carrying their script with me wherever I went. No matter where I was, I found myself trapped in the same narrative.

CRAFTING A NEW NARRATIVE

Working with motivation and theme is crucial for crafting a compelling new narrative that incorporates change. Shifting your motivations from fear to excitement and enthusiasm can transform your life experience. In the "What's Your Story?" section, I outline a process to help you uncover your life's pivotal themes and motivations, enabling you to rewrite your story with clarity and purpose.

Plot Points

To Recap:

- Lives have multiple themes: A single story isn't limited to one theme. Our lives are complex, and our experiences touch upon various underlying ideas. Motivations are often shared with many themes and can be a clue to others.
- Themes change**:** The themes that resonate most in your story might shift over time as you gain new experiences and reflect on your past with fresh perspectives.
- Motivations change: New perspectives and awarenesses allow us to examine and update motivations. Focusing on internal needs adds fulfillment in life.
- Uniqueness: Everyone's personal story is unique. The themes that emerge will be shaped by individual experiences and values.
- By exploring the themes in your personal stories, you unlock a deeper understanding of yourself and create a meaningful narrative that resonates with new, more fulfilling stories.

What's Your Story?

In my experience, I've found that life unfolds with rich and ever-evolving themes, yet a primary theme often sets the tone for the rest. Identifying the core theme can be crucial for understanding others. Exploring motivations is key to uncovering your central theme. Consider the process outlined below.

Step 1: Reflect on Your Life

Consider the experiences that have left the deepest imprint on you. What insights have you gained about yourself and the world? What obstacles have you conquered? Reflect on the choices you've made at different junctures and the reasons behind those decisions. In my line of work, it's common for a client to reveal that she pursued a career or college path because her parents did or because she wanted to follow in a parent's footsteps. If this choice brings her fulfillment, then it's perfectly valid. However, if she made the decision out of a sense of obligation, it's time to delve deeper.

Step 2: Find Patterns

Take on the role of an observer in your own life. Pay attention to the patterns that emerge. Recall a recent situation and replay it in your mind's eye. Imagine it as a scene unfolding on a stage. Notice your facial expressions, the tone of your voice, and your body language. What do you observe? Is this a common occurrence for you? Is your reaction typical? Now, pick another event and observe it in the same way. How does it connect to the first one? Are there any parallels or differences? Finally, select a third event and compare it to the first two.

When exploring career paths, focus on events related to your workplace or the tasks you perform. Ask yourself, "why this career or line of work?" Reflect on your interactions with colleagues, clients, and customers. Take note of any recurring themes or similarities and jot them down in a journal. What aspects were unexpected or surprising to you?

When looking at relationships, such as dating, look at the last three dates you were on. How did the dates unfold? What were the other people like? Did you like the other person but found that other person wasn't interested in you? If so, what transpired? How did you feel about not having your feelings returned? What emotion did that evoke? Compare the experiences. Is there a pattern? Do you say, "Why do I always attract this type of person?" Or, "Where are all the good ones?"

If it's relationships with friends or family, pick three interactions with the person you have the most energy around. Observe and note any patterns.

Step 3: Ask Why

When considering your behaviors and patterns ask yourself why. Why did you take an action? Why do you feel an emotion? Why is something important to you.? When you think you have the answer, ask why you had that answer. Then ask why again.

Step 4: What Matters Most

This step provides an opportunity to gain insight into the significance of leading a fulfilling life and leaving a meaningful legacy. I encourage any client to consider how she would feel upon receiving news of a limited time left to live. What does she believe others will remember about her? Does it align with her desired legacy? Reflect on experiences that bring genuine joy and areas of regret.

Dedicate time for reflection and document insights in a journal or recording. Dive deep into these reflections to foster heartfelt awareness. Seeking guidance from a trusted friend or coach throughout this process can be invaluable. When approached with care, any life has the potential to expand and evolve in surprising and unexpected ways.

By understanding and addressing your themes and motivations, you can gain insight into your actions and make intentional changes to your narrative. This awareness allows you to rewrite your story with a deeper understanding of the emotional drives behind your decisions, leading to a more empowered and authentic life.

6

Plot

It is not our abilities that show what we truly are … it is our choices.

— Dumbledore, *Harry Potter and the Chamber of Secrets*

September 1969—Seneca Junior High

My first day at Seneca Junior High School was also my first time on a school bus. The ride was bumpy and loud, filled with a mix of excitement and nervousness from all the students crowded onto the cracked fake leather seats. Anxiety oozed from the seventh and eighth graders not happy about the start of school. I hoped no one could sense the fears that started in my stomach and permeated through all the cells in my body.

Seneca buzzed with activity as buses lined the driveway, unloading students carrying bags and supplies. Half of us were new to the junior high experience, trying to find our way in this new environment.

With my schedule in hand, I followed the crowd into the school, looking for my locker and gym class. I found my homeroom and a desk with my name on it. I saw familiar faces from William Penn Elementary and my neighborhood. Donna Delveccio walked in and took a seat in the front row. I knew her, but we weren't friends. When our eyes met, she smiled, but it sent a chill down my spine. I knew she never liked me and had no idea why.

The first days turned into weeks. I adjusted to the rush between classes, the mountain of homework, and the awkwardness of changing for gym class. I liked phys ed but dreaded the showers, like most of the other girls who ran through them as quickly as possible to avoid prying eyes. If I could avoid the showers, homeroom, and Donna Delveccio, life would be good.

One morning, just as the holidays approached, my world fell apart. My bus was late, and I had to run to make it to homeroom. As I walked in, Donna called out, "Does anyone smell something awful?" The class erupted in laughter. Sherylle, Donna's friend, chimed in, "Yes! It smells like an old gym bag!" I wanted to crawl under my desk as the taunts continued until the teacher arrived. The next few days were a nightmare. My classmates pinched their noses when they saw me, singing songs about my hygiene, breath, and teeth. In the cafeteria, tables cleared when I sat down.

I was miserable and didn't want to go back to school. After a particularly bad day where the songs were louder, as it seemed like the entire student body joined in, I went home, crawled into bed and skipped dinner. Mom came into my room and switched on the light.

"I called you. Are you sick? We're ready to eat."

"I'm not hungry." I was curled in a ball, facing the wall. Mom put her hand on my forehead.

"You don't have a fever. What's wrong?"

"I'm not going back to school. The kids hate me and they're calling me names."

"You can't worry about those kids. They're just jealous." Mom's tone was sharp.

"Jealous of what? I don't have nice clothes or any friends. They hate me."

Mom's brief moment of tenderness vanished. "You're going to school. If you don't want dinner, you can do the dishes when you're done sulking." She left the room and turned off the light, leaving me alone in the dark.

PLOT: THE PROTAGONIST'S JOURNEY

The story from my junior high years, starting with "My Popcorn Story" from the chapter on Story Arc, reflects a persistent feeling of being alone and in danger. Mom's reactions to my challenges consistently lacked compassion and empathy throughout my adolescence. Later, I realized she treated all my siblings the same way, which, admittedly, made me feel less alone. All of these factors contribute to the next part of storytelling: the plot.

Once characters are introduced, themes and motivations established, and the inciting incident revealed, we move to the protagonist's journey. The plot, a series of events driving the story from start to finish, takes center stage. Think of the plot as the vehicle navigating a story map, guiding characters through various parts of their journey. The plot is always driven by the underlying theme it supports.

When I examined my life story, I realized it was dominated by a theme of trauma and constant fear. The bullying I endured in school and the lack of a safe, loving environment perpetuated this plot. The bullying escalated, forcing me to confront my fears without the skills or support of a caring family. Like fictional plots, personal plotlines also have thematic focuses. My theme was survival, vividly displayed during junior high.

Reflecting on that time now, I see it as a testament to my strength and determination. Changing my perspective allowed me to feel empowered instead of victimized. This shift in viewpoint, a vital storytelling technique for healing and rewriting personal narratives, is something I explore in a later chapter.

In personal stories, plots differ from those in fictional narratives. Fictional plots are often linear, with the protagonist moving step-by-step toward resolution. Personal plots, however, twist and turn, revealing interconnected events that might seem separate at first glance. These connections can be hard to see when you're in the thick of it. Working with a coach or therapist can help you see the broader picture.

Personal stories contain multiple simultaneous plots, each supporting different themes. This complexity enriches life's overall narrative. We juggle careers, relationships, personal growth, and hobbies, each with their own subplots. As I grew to understand the various stories I was living simultaneously I was amazed, as it highlighted the resilience and beauty of the human experience.

When I examined my career story, I saw a theme of lack, which drove me to seek high-paying but unfulfilling jobs. Career satisfaction didn't matter; I just wanted the money.

Initially, my theme of survival seemed separate from my theme of lack, but untangling these two plotlines revealed just how my professional challenges were linked to my survival theme and explained my deep unhappiness. Understanding these connections helped me to see how my past shaped my present and guided me toward rewriting a more fulfilling future.

THE PLOT THICKENS

When working with the plot of a personal story, you often notice repeated events. Clients frequently tell me, "Why do I always date the wrong guy?" or, "My co-workers never include me. It's like that in every job I've had." These patterns are the biggest clue to the story's plot. The core of each plotline centers on the challenges faced, both internal and external. This is the area to focus on when looking to write a new chapter for your life.

In my journey of rewriting my life story, I started with the same narrative but examined my challenges with an eye on what I gained from the experience. Instead of focusing on my classmates' cruelty, I saw my courage in going to school every day and trying out for cheerleading. I redefined my story with a theme of determination and resilience.

With this new theme, I viewed myself as a winner who persevered against the odds and created a fulfilling life. Recognizing and reinterpreting these patterns allowed me to shift my narrative from one of struggle to one of triumph.

Plot Points

To Recap:

- The plot captures the richness and complexity of your experiences.
- Each plot contributes to a different theme and shows different aspects of your growth and transformation.
- The plot is the vehicle for the protagonist's journey.
- In personal stories, a plot can have multiple twists and turns that may seem disconnected but are actually an important part of how you function in a story.

What's Your Story?

The plot is about the events of life. In your personal story, the plot is repetitious. What you did today, you will probably do tomorrow and the next day. Sometimes, the plot can stretch out, with events being weeks, months, or even years apart. Knowing this upfront will help you discover the plot of your story.

Step 1: Choose a life story

What story do you tell yourself that you want to change? Do you seek more happiness, stronger relationships, a new career path, or the pursuit of a long-held passion? To start, take a moment to center yourself. Take a few deep breaths and pay attention to the voice in your mind that keeps distracting you. It could be about a work project or a task at home. These thoughts are clues to the stories that need your attention. Once you identify the recurring story in your mind, you'll know where to begin.

Step 2: Patterns

Story in hand, look for the patterns. What challenges or struggles have you experienced multiple times in this story? If it's a relationship story, perhaps you're struggling with a family member and a problem that's existed for years. In your career, do you repeatedly feel passed over for promotions or do you always have conflicts with others on your team? Write down any patterns you find.

Step 3: Frequency

Now that you have a list, note how often this occurs. Is this something that's been going on for years? Is it the same every time, or are there nuances? In my stories, it was the ongoing issue of feeling unsafe.

Step 4: Look at the story from a different perspective

Shift your perspective and take responsibility for this situation. This plot you're living in is designed to bring you to a place where you become a better person. With that in mind, see something about yourself that you hadn't noticed before. When I first did this, I saw my determination. In your story, look at your commitment to being a better person. Notice that you're willing to resolve the issue by taking responsibility for your part in the narrative.

Step 5: Take back your power

You are not a bad person, nor are the others involved terrible. Forgive them and yourself for being part of this story. This will give you new insights into who you are and the narrative that's been playing out. The goal is to stop reacting to old patterns and recognize that you can respond differently. Over time, the plot will shift as you continue to make new choices.

7

Point of View and Perspective

> When you get a different vantage point, it changes your perspective ... It allows us to see things that maybe we should have seen a long time ago.
>
> — Neil Armstrong, *First Man*

January 1972

John H. Litton Intermediate School was busy. The school opened in time for my freshman year of high school, and it was the first of its kind in the state. The offices had glass walls with drapes that could be closed for privacy. The hallways were broader than those of a typical high school, and the new floors and lockers were an upgrade from those at Seneca. Litton Intermediate taught the ninth and tenth graders in the Penn Hills school district. Officials for the Department of Education were often onsite for events like the one taking place that day, which happened to be College Day.

Tenth graders held pamphlets and notebooks and gathered in the hallway near the offices as they waited for their turn to meet with counselors. I waited in line with all the other Advanced Placement students. I wore my best slacks and shoes that I'd cleaned the night before. My long dark hair was pulled back in a ponytail. I wore blush, eye shadow, and mascara that I kept tucked away in my room, away from Mom's prying eyes. I reapplied the lip gloss that I carried in my bag and hoped I looked okay. I wanted to make a good impression after the challenges of these last three years.

It had started with the bullying from Donna Delveccio and her pals, and then Sally had ruined my chances of joining the cheerleading squad. The eighth grade was just as bad. I befriended a girl who was ostracized by the other kids at school. She was bullied like I was for reasons that didn't make sense to me. When I tried to talk to Mom about it, she just told me that Jackie was a "bad girl" and I should stay away from her. But I didn't have any friends, and Jackie wanted me to be her friend. I jumped at the chance. Jackie hung out with two boys, Richard and Jerry, most evenings. I wasn't allowed out at night and longed to find a way to sneak out. It wasn't until the spring that I found out I'd made a mistake. I learned what being a "bad girl" meant when I went to my locker and saw that someone had painted "SLUT" across the door. I was devastated. To make matters worse, I was ambushed by a group of girls between classes. They surrounded me. One of them, Jennifer, came forward and told me to stay away from her boyfriend or else. I was frozen on the spot. They stared at me for what seemed an eternity and walked away laughing.

Their harassment continued through the end of eighth grade. That summer, desperate for friends, I continued my contact with Jackie while anxiously awaiting the new school year, hopeful for some relief after a horrible two years. It didn't happen. The new school was beautiful but the same people who hated me were still there. Jennifer didn't waste any time, using her friends to call me out for a fight. I felt the familiar dread every morning. I told Mom, hoping for any advice. All she said was to ignore the girls.

One day it all came to a head. By that time, half my class knew about Jennifer and her accusations that I had stolen her boyfriend. I figured it out when I realized that one of the boys that Jackie hung out with back at Seneca Junior High was, in fact, Jennifer's boyfriend. So, there I was, guilty by association.

Jennifer had approached me at the new school just as Litton was showcased for its advanced education offerings. Several officials were visiting, and the school was in tip-top shape to welcome the guests. Jennifer confronted me in front of the offices. I tried to walk away, but she grabbed my shirt and threw me to the ground. What happened next was a blur, but a teacher separated us and dragged us to the office. We were both suspended for the week.

Now, a year later, I sat in the same spot, in front of the offices, waiting.

A door opened, breaking my reverie. Miss Wilkins stepped out and said, "Carrie Powell, Jeannette Williams, and Joseph Carvey, please step forward." I walked with the others to where Miss Wilkins stood. She led us into the offices and directed each of us to individual rooms.

I entered the room Miss Wilkins indicated and found Mr. Barlow sitting at the desk. Mr. Barlow was my sixth-grade teacher. I'd heard he was promoted to a counselor in middle school and visibly relaxed when I saw the familiar face across from me. He had my file open and pointed to the chair. I sat and said, "Hi, Mr. Barlow! How are you?"

He looked at me and said, "I'm well, Carrie. I've been looking at your files and have to say, when you left William Penn, I thought I'd be hearing exciting things about you. And now when I read your file, I'm disappointed. What happened to you?"

I wanted to crawl under the desk. I looked down at my hands wondering if I was doomed to a failed life. "I hated Seneca. It was awful. But last year, the counselor told me the only way I'd get into college was to get my grades up. I've done that."

Mr. Barlow nodded. "Yes, you have. But they have to stay this way and even higher. I see this year, so far, you have straight A's, but last year was a mixed bag. Your seventh and eighth grades were awful—low C's. You need the A's to get into a decent school. At this point, I was hoping I'd recommend a top school like Yale or Brown. But now, I'm not sure."

My heart sank. I'd researched schools and wanted to get out of Pennsylvania, as far away from my family as possible. Even with Sally at Pitt, my life at home was miserable. "What do you think are my best options?"

Mr. Barlow took a deep breath and sat back in his chair. "Maybe Pitt, maybe Penn State if you get the grades. And then there are the SATs. They're set for next month. What are you thinking of for a major?"

All I wanted was a chance to get away. "I haven't thought about a major."

Mr. Barlow pursed his lips. "When I had you in class, I saw so much potential. To see you fall so far off the path disturbs me deeply. You were always so good at math. Does engineering or any of the sciences appeal to you?"

They didn't, but I didn't want to disappoint Mr. Barlow again. "I guess so. I thought about being a doctor or a veterinarian."

That seemed to appease him. "Good. Excellent. There are a lot of schools and programs that are looking for girls to go into the sciences. I'm going to suggest you take a strength assessment test that will give us a better idea. I'll schedule something for next week." He made a note in my file.

I waited until he was finished. "Mr. Barlow, there are some schools here in the auditorium that I want to talk to. I was hoping to study out of state. Are you saying I shouldn't bother?"

He thought about it for a minute. "Not necessarily, now that I know pre-med is an option. I know you're a smart girl, and I can even write you a recommendation. But if you have your heart set on somewhere, we must start planning now. After you visit the schools here, set up another time to meet with me." He folded my file and set it on the side of his desk. The meeting was over.

I went to the auditorium and saw several schools with desks and banners proudly displayed. The usual Pennsylvania schools took up over half the space. In addition to Pitt and Penn State, there was Carnegie Mellon, Temple, Villanova, Indiana University,

Duquesne, Slippery Rock, and some other less familiar names. I strode by them, looking for the out-of-state colleges. I found the State University of New York (SUNY), Ohio State, Michigan, Notre Dame, and one that caught my eye: the University of California.

When I arrived home that afternoon, I went straight to the room I shared with Tessa and closed the door. I reached between the mattresses and pulled out a journal and grabbed my pen.

"Today, I saw what it would be like to live and study at a college in California. The photos of the campus were gorgeous, sunny, green, and with clear blue skies. I talked to the counselors from the University of California, and it sounded perfect. And it's on the other side of the country. I'd finally be free of all this shit. Mom and Dad would never come to see me in California! When I was little and couldn't sleep at night, I dreamed of living in California in my own large, sunny, and beautiful home. Maybe, just maybe, I can go to school there, and I'll have my dream come true. Maybe."

HOW DOES OUR PERSPECTIVE IMPACT US?

In this story, I write about the trauma I endured in junior high school and how it affected my dreams of going to college. It's told from my point of view, which is the topic of this chapter and the next step in working with your personal story.

Point of View (POV) is the storyteller's voice that tells the story's events. The most common types are first-person and third-person voices:

First-Person POV: The narrator lives the story, sharing events from her perspective—for example, my narration of the tale above.

Third-Person POV: The narrator exists outside the events, describing characters' behaviors using names and pronouns like he, she, or they.

Perspective, on the other hand, is the storyteller's inner thoughts and interpretation of what is happening in the story. This unique lens is shaped by the narrator's background, experiences, values, and biases, adding her emotions and motivations to the narrative.

A storyteller's perspective influences how events are presented, what details are included, and the emotional impact the story has. Think about when a friend calls to gripe about someone she is dating. She shares her side, portraying herself as the wronged party. A few days later, the boyfriend tells his side, and it's a different story altogether. In my story above, the time in high school was very painful for me. That pain seeps through when I tell the stories of the bullying and my interactions with Jennifer.

I often tell my clients, "Everything is neutral; you put a spin on it." This means that while events are neutral, your mind, experiences, and stories determine the impact. Themes color the spin and your responses to life's events.

For example, I've discussed important events with my sister, Tessa, many times. Her recollections often differ slightly from mine, highlighting the importance of perspective. If she had told my stories from her point of view, readers might have a different impression. I sometimes sought Tessa's perspective while working through my healing and rewriting my story. Despite being nineteen months younger, she remembered many of our infancy stories and felt shame for what Mom said and did to me. If Tessa had written this story, she might have added elements of pity or sorrow on my behalf.

As you rewrite your story, consider different perspectives. It's crucial to understand the viewpoints of other characters in the story. Looking at an event from another person's point of view can allow you to focus on your strength and determination by reframing the experiences that hold you back.

THE PLOT THICKENS

Changing perspectives impacts your emotions. Your emotions arise from how you interpret events. For example, two people stand on the sidewalk when a car races by. One of them thinks, "That's so scary! That driver is a danger to us and should be arrested!" The other person frowns and thinks, "Oh, my! That driver is in such a hurry! I hope his family is okay. Why else would he drive like that? He must be really worried!" Each person had a different perspective that affected her emotions. The first person became angry, while the second person was concerned.

This example demonstrates that your filters, themes, and experiences shape your perspective. Shifting that perspective changes the lens through which you view an event, leading to different interpretations and new emotional responses.

By actively changing your perspective, you create a narrative that highlights your resilience and capability, replacing feelings of victimhood with empowerment and pride. This adjustment builds a positive self-image and reinforces your belief in your ability to navigate future challenges.

Plot Points

To Recap:

- Point of view is an important next step in working with a story.
- Shifting perspective empowers feelings of confidence and builds a belief of strength in yourself.
- The concept that, "Everything is neutral; you put the spin on it" expands the idea of working with perspective and opens the door to a new understanding of life's events.

What's Your Story?

Here's how you can revise the perspective of your story:

Step 1: Acknowledge Your Filters

Recognize that your story is filtered through your personal lenses, shaped by your issues, themes, motivations, and emotions. Remember, "Everything is neutral; you put the spin on it."

Step 2: Identify a Repeated Story

Think of a story you've told and lived repeatedly. Write about the events and how they affected your life in your journal. Tell the story in the first person, using your voice and your point of view. You can refer to the stories I've shared about the bullying I experienced in junior high school as examples.

Step 3: Retell as an Observer

Rewrite the story from an observer's point of view, describing the details without ascribing any emotions to them. This helps remove the emotional charge from the situation. Remember, "Everything is neutral; you put the spin on it."

For example, here's a neutral version of a bullying story: "I went to school every day. Kids in homeroom pinched their noses and said I smelled bad. During the day, others made comments in the hallway. When I sat down in the cafeteria, kids walked away. In ninth grade, Jennifer followed me around with her friends every day. One day, I saw her standing in front of the office with her friends."

Step 4: Neutralize the Emotions

Read the neutral story several times. If any emotions come up, continue until you can read it without any feelings arising. The key is to take the energy, the charge off the story so that you can reach understanding of the events from a new perspective.

Step 5: Explore the Antagonist's Perspective

Identify the antagonist in your neutral story and retell it from their perspective.

For instance, from Jennifer's perspective: "Nothing ever goes my way. How dare she steal my boyfriend? I heard from Donna Delveccio that she chased him and asked him out. I hate her. What if he thought she was cuter than me? I have to do something, or my friends will think I'm a loser. Carrie is smart and will go to college and have a great life. I need to find a husband and get out of my shitty house."

Seeing the story from Jennifer's perspective reveals her pain and insecurities, making forgiving and moving on easier.

Step 6: Consider Other Perspectives

If there are other characters in the story, such as another antagonist, a foil, or a mentor, write the story from their perspective as well. Review these versions to see if new insights emerge.

In my life, I learned that my parents were broken people with their own issues. While I didn't know any of this as a child, discovering how their situation impacted the story I developed in my life gave me perspective. I saw them as people before they were parents. It allowed me to forgive them and set myself free.

Step 7: Reflect on Your Feelings

Notice any new feelings that arise with this awareness. It might take time for these new perspectives to fully make sense. Be patient and try to enjoy the process.

Step 8: Seek External Input

Working with a coach or therapist can help you see the story from someone else's perspective. Consider engaging with a coach or therapist to help build a new understanding, which can lead to acceptance of the new narrative.

By following these steps, you can shift your perspective and transform the way you understand and tell your life story.

8

Repeating Chapters – Staying Stuck

You know how it is. You like what you're used to.

— Lord Grantham, *Downton Abbey*

September 1981

I returned Tessa's call first. She was distraught and said, "Where have you been? Something awful has happened! Mark was off-duty and shot and killed a man! He's going to jail. Mom and Dad are freaking out!" My jaw tightened; my body went rigid. Was it to brace myself for the next onslaught of words that Tessa threw my way? My confused mind wanted to make sense of what she was saying. I could not. The rapid-fire bad news didn't give me a chance to breathe. I tried to focus on how happy my brother Mark was when he got the job with the Allegheny County Police and hoped it was a chance for him to have the life he wanted.

I couldn't feel anything, not even the phone in my hand. I was at the office, sitting in an open area with desks and people on phones, but I heard nothing and saw nothing around me. After an eternity, I felt the phone's weight in my hand and said, "Tessa, I have to call you back. Two minutes." I hung up and walked quickly towards the conference room.

David, the office manager, saw the look on my face and said, "What's wrong?"

"I need to make a private call. It's about my family," I said. I walked into the conference room, closed the door, and took a few deep breaths. I looked for and found a bottle of water. I grabbed it and took a sip or two. Then I dialed Tessa.

"Tell me everything," I said when Tessa answered.

Tessa relayed the events from the previous weekend. "Mark was driving back from a party. There was a crowd around Three Rivers Stadium and some commotion after a football game. Mark was stuck, so he got out of his truck to see what was happening. He saw a crowd of people around the cars. He said it looked like there'd been an accident. People were arguing, and it looked like it would get out of hand fast. Mark went back to his car, grabbed his gun, and fired a warning shot."

I could see the scene unfold as Tessa spoke. Mark, always the cowboy, wanted to be a police officer more than anything. Protect and Serve—the police motto was Mark's motto. Only Mark's notion of protect and serve gave him a sense of power over situations he wasn't designed to handle. When he joined the force, I thought that time would tell how it would play out. I knew I shouldn't be shocked at Tessa's words, but I had hoped the work would give him a chance to mature into someone that maybe he wasn't.

Tessa said that at the sound of the gun, the crowd dispersed, got in their cars, and things started to move. Mark went back to his car, drove to his apartment, then called police headquarters to report that he'd fired his gun off-duty, as was policy. He went to bed only to be awakened the next morning by a call from someone from his squad saying that a man had died from the warning shot after it hit a light post and ricocheted into the man's chest. It was a freak accident, but Mark was taken into custody and had to explain the events of the night before. He was placed on leave and advised not to return to his apartment because the press was all over the story. Instead, Mark went to our parents.

I hung up the phone and took a breath to calm myself before calling Mom and Dad. I wanted more than anything to be someone else, anywhere else, than where I was that very moment. I looked around the well-appointed conference room with the beautiful wooden credenza and the papered walls with plaques awarded to the office for its success. Just as I felt like I was finally on track to make something of my life, the last two months had shown me otherwise. First, my apartment building in Silver Spring, Maryland, burned down. Joe, the man I was dating, let me stay with him after the fire, but it quickly became clear that he was a nasty alcoholic. Seeking clarity, I went away for a weekend to process everything, and that's when Mark's shooting happened.

I picked up the phone and dialed.

Dad answered, something he never did. I took a moment to settle. "Hi, it's Carrie. What happened?"

I listened as Dad relayed almost the same information I heard from Tessa. When he was done, I said the words I had hoped never to say again. "I've got to sort out some things here, but then I'm coming home. I'll let you know when."

Dad's response should have shocked me, but it didn't. "Sally's coming and said she'd take care of everything. You don't have to make the trip from Maryland if you don't want to." I sat with my head in one hand and the phone in the other.

"If you don't want me there, I won't come." The pain in my heart throbbed. Would they ever stop rejecting me?

There was a sound on the line, and my mother's voice said, "You have to come home! Mark needs you. He's your brother. You have to be with your family!"

I took some time off work and went to my parents' house in Pittsburgh. When I arrived, the whole family was there. Mom was hysterical. Dad was more withdrawn than ever. Mark sat around looking like a victim. Sally was there with her two young daughters.

While my parents were in deep pity, Sally, who was married to a television director and working in the film industry, promised justice and would pay for the best attorney. I observed Mark and could not help but think that this tragic event was not a surprise. Mark often talked about going to Vietnam to kill some "gooks" and would pull out his gun when I drove him home at night, aiming at people on the street, mostly people of color. More than once I threatened to drop him off in the worst neighborhoods if he didn't hide his goddamn guns.

Mark looked contrite, even a bit shocked at events that were unfolding around him. I thought he finally knew what it felt like to take a human life. I wondered if it compared to him hunting deer but didn't say anything. He was in enough trouble with the newspapers calling for his head and the family being dragged through the mud. The neighbors were silent, and Mom had to keep her head up when she went out. Dad was terrified for his only son. After a couple of days, I returned to Maryland. All in all, 1981 was turning out to be a crappy year.

I found a new apartment and cleared up all the insurance issues. I even bought a car because I had a feeling I'd be going to Pittsburgh quite a bit over the next few months. Owning a car would be more cost-effective than renting one.

Mark's trial was in April 1982. He was found guilty of voluntary manslaughter. I missed the trial but went to the sentencing, where he was sentenced to no more than five years in prison. They took him straight to the county jail to await transport to a prison near Penn State. I felt so much shame and humiliation coming from such a poor family and now having this burden to bear. Mom cried out in the courtroom. Dad surprisingly held Mom and took my hand. He got us in the car and drove home while Mom sobbed about losing her boy. I felt alone and isolated in a horrible dream I could not wake up from.

I was grateful to return to Maryland. No one there knew about my family's shame, and I could get back to work with relative ease. But I drank a lot and was flirting more with men, even if they were married. After I made a mess of things with one prospective job candidate, his wife threatened to call my boss. I decided it was time to leave Maryland and everything that had happened when I moved there. The fire, my relationship with Joe, my brother... I had to run away. I moved back to Pittsburgh for an extended stay to deal with the fallout from my brother. Mom was afraid to leave the house for fear of what people were saying, and Dad wasn't in much better spirits. While in Pittsburgh, I met with a recruiting firm to make some money during my stay. It turned out that they were in the process of opening an office in Northern Virginia on the other side of Washington DC. I jumped at the chance. It not only got me out of my parents' house, but it also got me away from the mess I'd made in Maryland.

Sally had a falling out with our parents shortly after Mark went to prison. She had hired a prominent and expensive attorney, then forced Mom and Dad to take out a second mortgage on their home to pay her back. Sally was pregnant with her third child, and so Dad decided to make sure he took care of Sally even if he lost his favored son to what he called "unfair circumstances." Dad's heart was broken. I watched him withdraw into his anger and pain at how his son had turned out, convinced that Mark's life was over.

When Sally gave birth to a boy in early November, Dad went to the hospital to see his new grandson. Sally didn't turn him away; she never would. Instead, she forgave Dad for whatever wrong she felt had been done to her and said she'd bring the baby by right after Thanksgiving. Sally and her family had planned to spend Thanksgiving with her husband Will's family in Ohio. They'd stop by on the way back.

STAYING STUCK IN OUR STORIES

Stories reveal something amiss in your life and how the issue began in the first place. I discovered it each time I looked at my life and how I functioned. As shared in the above story, I was unsettled, floundering with no sense of self or purpose. It was yet another story that showed I hadn't fully escaped my family's drama. I felt that I was an integral character in their play, as they were in mine. Without a career that I loved, I jumped from job to job. I accepted the contract or work assignment as long as I was paid well. I tolerated the work because I needed the money. Or I could escape whatever mess I'd made with the previous assignment. When I decided to examine my life, I read books about doing what I loved, and the money would come. Only I had no idea what I loved except having enough money to survive.

I wasn't successful in relationships, romantic or otherwise. Strong relationships require trust, first with yourself and then from the people around you. My experiences as a child taught me I wasn't safe, so I was guarded for fear I'd be hurt. Even determining where I wanted to live was a challenge, so I moved from state to state until I finally moved to California in my mid-thirties, finally fulfilling a dream of mine to attend graduate school at the American Film Institute.

Looking at these experiences as an observer, I found that the stories I told in those earlier days were filled with angst and self-pity, masking my rage and pain. The experience with my brother going to jail was a continuation of the same pain and angst I had felt for as long as I could remember. When I started journaling, I realized that nothing had changed.

I kept auditioning and winning roles for the "Third Born Middle Child" or the "Not Wanted" character. It reminded me of the scripts from film school, where the throwaway parts were often labeled "Student in Back Row" or "Drunk Male at the Bar." Sometimes, my parts were brief, sometimes epic, and sometimes, I gave Oscar-worthy performances. But they were the same. Even when I thought I'd left the stage behind, the script, theme, and characters all came with me, or rather, I found the stories that matched the character actor I was.

Many people have the same experience. After being told something repeatedly, we start to believe it is the truth. No matter how long it has been since the original story started, the worn and tattered script ends up in your back pocket, ready to be pulled out and read at a moment's notice.

Some women, me included, look for and date men who are like our fathers. Call it something known and comfortable, or being drawn to the familiar. My entire dating experience consisted of falling for the "bad boys." They were cute and had long hair and fast cars. I cried over them, I wrote about them in my journals, and I wrote my name over and over as "Mrs. Badboy." I tried to win them over and prove I was lovable and great if they would only give me a chance.

My further investigation led me to the deeper pain and the lack of deserving I felt. It went back to the very beginning when, to make sense of this drama in my life, I created a story that blamed me for my parents' problems. As with any epic story, there are several plots, twists, and turns. Feeling that I was responsible for my parents' happiness was one of the threads of the story that touched other plots and subplots, repeatedly making me think I didn't deserve anything better than the "bad boys." Resolving all the plots meant I would finally fill this wide hole in me that was a key focus of my life. But there really wasn't a hole. What I really wanted was to prove I deserved my family's love.

A great definition of insanity is doing the same thing repeatedly and expecting different results. This is the perfect message for this chapter. Recognizing what isn't working so you can change direction is the next step in writing a new story. Staying stuck in old narratives means missing opportunities for new futures. It's easy to overlook helpful opportunities because your attention is elsewhere.

When I began working on my stories, I realized how much I loved writing, recalling the journals I kept as a teenager. After Mom died and I cleaned out her house, I found some of those journals. As a teenager, I had several career ideas: I wanted to be an astronaut when men were landing on the moon, and an engineer because they earned $1,000 a month, which seemed like a fortune. The dream that stuck with me was becoming a famous writer. But how could I achieve that if I kept living my life as the poor truck driver's daughter?

THE PLOT THICKENS

In the movie "Groundhog Day," Bill Murray plays an egotistical, entitled weatherman who thinks he deserves better than what he's getting in life. He's charming enough but complains to everyone, especially when he finds himself in situations he thought were beneath him. Act Two starts with him waking up on the same day as before, February 2nd, and we're off on this funny, poignant movie, watching this character rewrite his story right before our eyes. For the first several repeated days, he tries everything to end his misery, but doing what he always did: demand, complain, bully. It was the very definition of doing the same thing repeatedly and expecting a different result. "Groundhog Day" metaphorically shows how most people live the same day, repeating old patterns and hoping for a better outcome.

There are several reasons for repeating chapters and plots in your story.

- Unresolved trauma
- Fear and resistance to change

- Lack of a support system
- Lack of understanding
- Guilt

UNRESOLVED TRAUMA

If you're a twelve-year-old boy in junior high and you trip and fall in front of a bunch of kids, they'll probably laugh, and you'll feel like an idiot. By the end of the day, the fall will be mostly forgotten, and you'll return to your life. Let's say you're that same twelve-year-old boy and you trip, but you do it in front of a kid in your class that doesn't like you. When he sees you fall, he takes the chance to humiliate you by saying something cruel, calling you a name, and then inciting the crowd to do the same. This bully gives you the nickname of "Grace." The other kids love it and start calling you Grace. They write it on your locker, they make up a song, and this bully keeps the humiliation going on for what seems like an eternity in your twelve-year-old brain. You dread going to school, a place you once loved. Your grades fall, and as the bullying increases and grows into new areas, you stop eating and fall into a deep depression. This experience is traumatic.

Now, forty years later, you start a new job. Your boss' name is Grace. For some reason, you don't get along with her. She's a good boss and nice enough. She treats you well. But at night, you're restless, losing sleep. You sleep in a couple of times and are late. Then, your work suffers because your concentration slips. Grace calls you in to talk, and you shake uncontrollably. On the surface, it makes no sense at all. But when you look at what happened to that twelve-year-old, it makes perfect sense. Even though your boss, Grace, didn't humiliate you, the name "Grace" is the triggering event that brought up all the buried, unexpressed feelings from your twelve-year-old self.

This happened to one of my clients. It was a traumatic experience that forced him to leave a job that was perfect for him and one that he loved. It was also an opportunity to uncover the trauma, heal it, and move forward. He did so and found another job that was perfect for him. Along with the awareness of his trauma, he healed and became a happier person all around.

Everyone has experienced a trauma. Unresolved trauma causes the kind of stress and fear that keeps you from leading a full life. In a natural state, you think before you react. In a stressed state, you can't. That means you can be provoked at any time in your life. Sometimes, it shocks you, and you suddenly start shaking and feeling anxious. Sometimes you feel fear without any logical reason. Trauma interrupts your natural awareness, making you feel disconnected and keeping you stuck in dilemmas.

Triggering events, common in unresolved traumas, engage the lizard brain—the amygdala—which then releases chemicals to prepare for a fight-or-flight response. Once the threat is over, the brain recovers, and life continues. Sometimes, like my client above, the trauma continues. The replay is a retraumatizing event that continues the chemical outpouring from the amygdala. These drain the adrenal glands and affect the internal organs, sleep patterns, and well-being.

Until I realized and accepted the impact trauma had on my life, I risked being triggered at any time. When it happened, I got what I call a psycho-sensation of pain that's not physical, yet deeply and thoroughly mentally and emotionally stressful. My breathing became shallow, and I could not move. It also brought up fear – another aspect of trauma that has negative effects on life.

FEAR—RESISTANCE TO CHANGE

For many people, nothing is scarier than change. Change can be seen as a difficult undertaking and, therefore, to be avoided. One of the biggest fears is of the unknown. Not knowing what lies on the other side of a challenge or obstacle is frightening.

There are many situations where it's easier to stick with the status quo rather than face the fear of the unknown:

Toxic workplace—You might be asking yourself, "What if a new job is no better than where I am now?"

Malaise with your current job—Feeling stuck in a boring job without motivation to search for a new one is a common experience. Sometimes, it's easier to blame the timing of looking for a new career. There are bills to pay and families to support that justify the avoidance. This can be an expression of fear of change.

Relationships—The fear of being alone is a powerful reason often used to stay in unhealthy relationships. Plus, the impact on families and friends when you end a relationship often justifies a reason to stay.

Sometimes, changing a situation might be impossible due to various other considerations, such as a health crisis (yours or a family member's) or loss of financial support. But that doesn't mean there aren't options. Take a moment and see your experience as a crisis that holds an opportunity, something I'll explore in the next chapter. When this happens, taking responsibility for what led to unhappiness is one approach. Another is to look at the situation from a new perspective. These can bring a new attitude that inspires new ideas and actions.

Fear can be a powerful force that keeps you clinging to the familiar, even when it's not necessarily good for you.

LACK OF A SUPPORT SYSTEM

Rewriting your story doesn't have to be a solitary undertaking. In fact, having a support system can make all the difference in the journey. A coach, therapist, or trusted friend can act as an accountability partner. They can help you stay focused on your goals, celebrate your wins, and gently nudge you back on track when you stumble. They can also offer a new perspective when stuck old stories are playing in your head.

By involving support in your story's rewrite, you gain guidance, encouragement, and help when navigating challenges, staying motivated, and creating a new, fulfilling narrative.

LACK OF UNDERSTANDING

When embarking on a new story, I first like to remember that "it's an inside job." This is a powerful truth about taking responsibility for one's life. Always starting with an internal assessment of the current story and comparing it to the desired goal establishes a starting point for the work.

All personal growth starts from within. It may seem easy to blame an external force, other people, or outside circumstances, but doing so steals your personal power. The first step in any change process is to acknowledge that you are in the situation; accept it and choose something different. Acceptance doesn't mean resignation or liking the situation. It means acknowledging reality without judgment and letting go of resistance. This frees up energy for moving forward.

Motivation is also an "inside job." It's the "why" behind the decisions that lead to actions.

GUILT

Guilt is a complex and debilitating emotion. Excessive or prolonged guilt can lead to low self-esteem and staying stuck in old patterns. Guilt results from actions that harm or are thought to harm others. Sometimes, guilt comes from inaction in the face of a potentially difficult situation. Guilt is often used to mask other uncomfortable emotions like anger or sorrow. When dealing with guilt, look at the feelings underneath and release them. As I was starting to make real changes in my life, I found a pocket of guilt around the idea I was somehow breaking away from my family. What I found was that I was sitting on a great deal of rage that I thought could destroy anything in its way if I acknowledged it. Remember that it might be necessary to make amends and apologize to the harmed party. It's also important to forgive yourself and others involved. I offer forgiveness techniques in the chapter called "Turning the Page." Understanding guilt and its causes, and finding healthy ways to cope beyond feeling guilty, make it possible to move forward in rewriting the story.

Plot Points

To Recap:

- Most lives are repeats of scenes in old stories told over several years.
- Acknowledge the comfort of familiar patterns but emphasize the importance of stepping outside your comfort zone to explore new possibilities.
- People stay stuck in old stories for several reasons: unresolved trauma, fear, lack of support, lack of understanding, and guilt.
- Knowing where you fall on this list is valuable for changing your story.

What's Your Story?

When you're ready to stop writing the same chapter over and over in your journal, consider these steps:

Step 1: What do you want?

Start by recognizing your desire to rewrite your life story. What area do you want to work with? Career? Relationships? Overall happiness? Journaling and noting areas that you'd like to explore can help.

Step 2: Repeated Stories

Once you've chosen an area, think about the old stories that have been repeated. Is it about dating the same type of people who aren't great fits? Is it about working with a career that isn't satisfying?

Step 3: What Characters

List the characters of the story. Who is the antagonist? Who is the foil? Is there a best friend or love interest? List the most important roles and note who had the part.

Step 4: Where are you stuck?

Why hasn't anything been done to change the situation? Use the five reasons listed above to examine your resistance to change and determine which ones are behind the repetition of your stories.

Step 5: Compare to where you are today.

Write a sentence or two about how your resistance to change relates to your current situation.

Step 6: Reach for Understanding

Acknowledge that it is an inside job and that you are responsible. Practice feeling empowered by the knowledge that you are in charge of the situation and can make new decisions and choices.

Step 7: Forgiveness.

Forgiveness is a powerful force and an important one to remember. Forgiving yourself for any mistakes or problems sets you free. Sometimes, forgiveness seems impossible. At these times, I recommend forgiving the "why" someone acted as they did. I've given some examples and listed a couple of ways to forgive yourself and others in the chapter "Turning the Page."

Step 8: Unstuck – A New Chapter Begins

Now that you've worked through the steps listed here, it's time to put pen to paper. Write a new chapter describing how the new story unfolds. I recommend actually writing out your ideas in a journal or in a document file on your computer. In this new story, decide the following:

Characters—are they currently a part of your life or, if there are relationships you want to bring, then in write down the role they'll play in your life.

Dreams—what excites you or sparks your enthusiasm? Acknowledging this will inspire new motivations.

Ensure you have support by contacting a trusted friend, therapist, or coach for help. The support will help you through each of the steps.

This process may take some time to work through. Remember that this situation has been going on for some time. Changing your situation may not happen quickly but staying aware and present will make the transitions easier.

9

Conflicts, Crises, and Challenges

You're born to this shit. You are who you are.

— Tony Soprano, *The Sopranos*

November 1982

It was the Saturday after Thanksgiving. We sat watching television, Mom, Dad, and me. I was unsettled after a typical holiday and the usual complaints about what I was doing with my life and questions about when I would get married. I planned to leave in the morning and return to my apartment in McLean, Virginia. My co-worker, Roger— another Pittsburgher I was secretly in love with and wanted to date—was meeting me for the drive to Virginia. Roger was dating my roommate Judy, but that never bothered me before. I wanted Roger, and that was that. He was handsome and fun. I looked at my watch for the hundredth time, bored, waiting for anything to do before seeing Roger in the morning.

Just when I thought all was lost, the phone rang. A friend from college invited me to a party. I hung up the phone and said to the room, "Can I borrow the car? Carole is having a party, and I'd like to see her before I go back to DC."

Dad looked at me and said, "Get me a piece of pumpkin pie before you go. Put extra whipped cream on it." I took that as a yes, went into the kitchen, got a huge slice of pie, and slathered it in whipped cream, just the way I knew he liked it. I gave Dad the plate, burdened with the sweet, delicious pie, and went to my room to check my makeup and change my clothes. A short while later, I went back into the living room.

"Okay, I'm off. I don't know how late I'll be, but I have keys." Mom grunted. Dad, holding the half-eaten pie, put his fork on the plate and reached his hand toward me.

Taken aback by the gesture, I took his outstretched hand. Dad looked at me. "You know I love you, don't you?" In my twenty-four years, he'd never said those words to me. In my house, love was not something given freely and unconditionally. Love was something I was ordered to do, as in, "He's your brother. You have to love him."

I couldn't break his gaze, but an awful sensation came over me. Mom would have called this feeling someone walking on my grave. I pulled my hand away, shaken. "Yeah, Dad. I know. I'll see you later." I looked at him and saw something undefinable in his eyes. I turned and rushed out the door.

The restaurant Carole mentioned was by one of the rivers in downtown Pittsburgh. When I was near, not more than a couple of miles away, a pain shot through the side of my mouth. The pain was so intense and surprising that I almost ran a red light. I took a deep breath while stopped at the light. The pain lessened to a throb, so I continued to the restaurant. When I arrived, parked, and entered the front door, I noticed that the place was busy. Carole found me and signaled me to a corner where more friends sat. Just as I took a seat, the pain shot through my entire jaw, almost knocking me to the ground. Carole saw and asked. "Are you okay?"

I caught my breath. "I don't think so. I think I have to go. I am so sorry. I'll call you later this week."

I left. On the drive back to my parents, the pain lessened. For a moment, I thought about returning to the party but decided to go home and prepare to leave for DC. When I pulled into the driveway, I noticed three things: it hadn't been more than one hour since I'd left, and now there were three cars parked in front of the house. The pain in my jaw was gone. Instead, I felt a deep sense of dread.

When I walked in the door, Mom was sitting at the table. Dad's cousins Joe and Mary, and a couple of neighbors were sitting in the living room. Dad wasn't there. I looked around and tried to read the look on everyone's faces, but they just stared back. I looked at Mom and said, "Where's Dad?" My tone was sharp, but I knew that what Mom said next would break me. Instead, I looked at the dining room table near Mom. Dad's wallet, keys, and the coins he carried in his pockets were there. Again, I looked at Mom. "Where. Is. Dad?"

"He died. Twenty minutes after you left." She deadpanned. When I replayed this moment in my head later, I thought Mom made a great suffering widow. It suited her.

"You lying bitch!" The words came out before I could do anything about it. All the bottled-up emotions, anger, and pain coursed through my heart and soul and out of my mouth. Mom looked at me and put her hand up to the people in the room quieting them. Mom never looked so strong.

"Your father died tonight."

I stood facing Mom for a moment, then turned and walked down the hall into Dad's bedroom. He wasn't there. I knew he wouldn't be, but I couldn't accept that he wasn't.

Dejected, shocked with more emotions than I knew were possible, I walked back into the kitchen and grabbed the bottle of Canadian Club Whiskey that Dad kept on the shelf for when his paisanos stopped by for a shot or two. There was a large tumbler from the cheap set they bought with gas station promotional coupons on the shelf. I filled it with ice and then poured the whiskey. Mom watched. "You gonna drink that straight?" The glass was firmly in hand. I looked at Mom, grabbed the ginger ale, and tipped in a splash. The drink slid easily down my throat. I took another sip and another.

My breath came back to me. Steadied, I said, "Tell me what happened."

Mom told me that minutes after I left, Dad dropped the plate of pumpkin pie he was eating and grabbed his chest. Mom looked at him, his face gray, and asked if he was okay. He said to call the ambulance. Dad hated doctors. If he asked her to call an ambulance, this was bad. Very bad. The ambulance arrived within minutes and put Dad on a stretcher. As they went down the walkway, Dad yelled out, "Put me in a box and burn me. Bury my ashes over my mother's grave." When they got him in the ambulance, Mom saw the Emergency Medical Technicians trying to revive him. She called Joe and Mary and they took her to the hospital. He died before they got there. It was a coronary infarction, a term so strange sounding that I would have laughed at it before that night. Later, I found out that a coronary infarction meant that his heart just died.

Tonight, of all nights, he said he loved me—words I longed for, and now he was gone. Sleep escaped me. The next day, I called Tessa and Sally and then the prison where Mark was serving his sentence. Mom held court with all the sympathetic neighbors and friends that dropped by. Mom was in her power, accepting all the "Poor you" sympathy. Tessa caught a flight from Boston, and Sally and her family left Ohio. They would be there by the end of the day. Mark was another thing. The prison official said I had to pay to bring Mark to the funeral. We scheduled one showing for Wednesday so that Mark could be there after all the paperwork was processed. Food lost its appeal, and sleep was non-existent. The only thing I wanted was to stay busy and drink alcohol. Sally and Tessa sat with Mom and did whatever they did while I made arrangements and wondered why people were still functioning as if nothing had happened. Didn't they know the world had ended?

Dad wanted to be cremated, but the Catholic church was against cremation. The priest I knew from my early days of Catholicism, now aged and stooped, forbade us from burying Dad's ashes over *his mother's grave in a Catholic cemetery. Once he accepted a $200 donation, he gave us permission. Once the showing was arranged, the cremation and burial settled, there wasn't much for me to do except stare at all the people around me. And wait.*

Wednesday came. I'd never seen a dead body. Before the time when the doors were scheduled to open, I looked in the casket. Dad looked so peaceful in the sports jacket he wore at Sally's wedding. I touched his face. It felt stiff and dry.

Mark was due to arrive before the showing. He would be in shackles with a police escort. Mom wanted him there before anyone else so that she wouldn't be embarrassed. He arrived wearing a suit, handcuffed and with chains around his feet. He was sobbing and asked the guards to let him go so he could hug his mother. They refused, so Mom went to him and held him in her arms while he cried.

To his credit, Mark wanted to stay as long as possible. He didn't care who saw him. He took a seat between the guards on the side of the room. By noon, the place was full. People of all sizes and shapes, races, and genders came. Shock and awe filled me. My racist father had more than a few black men and women in attendance.

While people gathered and gave their sympathies to my family, I sat lost in my thoughts, remembering that moment when looking into his eyes, Dad told me he loved me.

Frank, my grandfather, arrived. He wept, sad that he was burying the last of his family. Mom's sisters showed up. Mom glowed as they all stood by her, making her the center of attention.

After some time passed, I took Tessa aside and said, "I need you and Sally to wrap things up. I sorted out Dad's finances and discovered Mom is getting money from the Teamsters and Dad's insurance policy. Apparently, he handled money better in death than he did in life."

"How so?" Tessa's shocked face fit her red, swollen, teary eyes.

"Dad's insurance will cover the mortgage they took out to pay for Mark's lawyers and the Teamsters are sending a check for $25,000.

Since he was sixty-two, he hasn't had any Social Security benefits, but with the cash and house, she'll be okay for a while. I just can't stay here any longer."

Tessa recovered and said, "Sure, sure. You did plenty. I'll call you later in the week."

Looking around the room, I saw that Sally sat with Mom, with Mark on Mom's other side. The deputies finally relented and gave him space. People came up to them, telling stories about Dad.

None of this made sense to me, so I left the room, got into the car I'd rented, and drove back to Virginia.

EMBRACING CONFLICT IN PERSONAL STORIES

Conflict is a crucial element in personal stories, just like it is in fiction. It's the friction that sparks growth, reveals our true nature, and offers clues about the person we've always been. My dad's death was one of the greatest crises I ever faced. From the shock of his passing to dealing with the aftermath, I was forced to make significant changes in my life. In hindsight, this crisis became a catalyst for extensive transformation.

In daily experiences, a crisis can be seen as a setback that gets in the way of something you desire or a goal you want to achieve. As illustrated previously, the teenage years are filled with conflicts and challenges as people form their identities and build their personal narratives. Adolescence, with its angst and turmoil, is a prime example of the role crisis plays in life. However, conflicts and crises aren't limited to teenage years; they also occur throughout adulthood. Whether it's the end of a relationship, starting a new job, or any other life change, viewing challenges as opportunities for growth makes transitions easier.

The pandemic brought new challenges for everyone. Entire industries changed, with remote and hybrid work becoming the norm. Many argue that it accelerated much-needed upgrades in business practices, especially through technological advances.

Conflict in personal stories can be internal, involving thoughts, emotions, and doubts that shape your responses. Addressing internal challenges requires self-awareness and a willingness to examine the repetitive stories in our minds. The difficulty lies not in hearing the story but in understanding the emotions it evokes. For instance, during my junior high years, I outwardly felt terror, loneliness, and isolation. I didn't consciously hear the negative narrative running in my head, but it convinced me I was unlovable and unlikable. My worth seemed tied to taking care of others at the expense of my needs and wants.

External conflicts arise from interactions with others, situations, or societal pressures. One of my junior high teachers viewed the bullying I endured as a rite of passage, something to grow from. While I eventually learned about my resilience, it took years of soul-searching and forgiveness to heal from those experiences.

Writing this book, filled with my personal story, was the most challenging task of my life. Even though I had worked with my story for decades, exposing my innermost anxieties publicly took this exploration deeper. It involved overcoming insecurities, stepping outside my comfort zone, and revealing my most intense vulnerabilities. This process made me feel freer than I ever have in my life.

Conflict also manifests itself in relationships with family and friends. My parents died long ago and my relationships with Sally and Mark didn't survive into adulthood. This unresolved pain influenced other relationships, creating a plot of mistrust and rejection. I discovered a longing for female friends, but my mother's rejection and Sally's animosity made me gravitate toward women who excluded or disliked me. This repeated plot of rejection led to challenges that I eventually overcame. I learned that not everyone would be a great friend, nor would I always want to be friends with everyone. Over time, I adjusted to the nuances of friendships and recognized the value I bring to them. More importantly, I found and cherished my own value.

It's easy to misunderstand the value of life's challenges, especially when you're in the thick of it. Reviewing both internal and external conflicts allows you to see your growth and create a narrative that resonates with a fulfilling life. Through these challenges, you emerge as a changed and empowered person, making your story more than just a recollection of events.

THE PLOT THICKENS

The idea that challenges and crises are opportunities is crucial. They serve as catalysts for positive change and growth in several ways:

Disruption of the Status Quo: Crises shake us out of our routines, forcing us to reevaluate our priorities, goals, and even our identities. This can be especially painful if the crisis involves the loss of a relationship or a loved one. For example, divorce, though initially overwhelming, can ultimately leave both parties stronger and in a better place.

Skill Development and Confidence Building: Overcoming obstacles equips us with new skills and the confidence to handle future challenges. Although this may not be apparent at the time, working through a crisis can lead to significant personal change. Many of my clients report feeling happier and even excited when they recognize the new possibilities that emerge as a result.

Innovation and Community Building: While devastating, natural disasters and catastrophes force people to adapt and find solutions, which can lead to new ideas and approaches that were previously unconsidered. Such events also unite communities, reminding us of our shared humanity during critical times.

Dealing with Uncertainty: Crises can be overwhelming, primarily due to the unknown. Humans are creatures of habit, and being forced out of our comfort zones can be frightening. The level of uncertainty varies based on the individual and the situation's severity. Seeking external support, such as working with a therapist or coach, is crucial during these times.

In my experience, while crises can be daunting and leave little room for optimism, they also present opportunities for great growth and transformation. Embracing these opportunities, despite the discomfort, can lead to new more fulfilling chapters in your life story.

Recognizing a crisis as an opportunity, especially in the midst of chaos, is challenging. Not all crises invite us to reconsider who we are, but many highlight what isn't working and where we can make shifts in our lives. Major life events, like marriage or having children, clearly indicate significant changes ahead, but often, these transitions come with time to prepare. However, some crises strike suddenly and demand immediate attention. Here are some clues that indicate a challenge is at hand:

Ultimatums: When faced with an ultimatum, such as "do this or else," it's an opportunity to make a growth choice rather than a fear choice. A fear choice maintains the status quo out of fear of the unknown. Instead, consider making a bold decision and taking a new path.

Quick and Sudden Change: Life can throw unexpected curveballs, such as a loved one taking a job in another state, unexpected pregnancies, health scares, or discovering a significant betrayal. The pandemic, for example, plunged the world into an ongoing crisis. More dramatically, a loved one's accident can permanently alter their life and yours.

Loss of a Significant Other: Losing a parent, partner, or someone significant can have a profound and lasting impact. After my dad died, I had to reexamine my life, which led me to the journey described in this book. Reflecting on my life's story in my late twenties, I realized my desire to write and live in England. Unsure of my next steps, I explored various educational programs and was eventually accepted into the creative writing program at the University of London.

I dreaded the call to my mom to share my decision. After Dad died, Sally took care of her, bringing Mom on vacation to Sally's family cabin. Surrounded by her grandchildren and Sally, Mom thrived on the attention. But after a year, Sally grew tired and decided that Mom wasn't worth the effort. Feeling lost and abandoned, Mom leaned on me more than ever. She went from being a cared-for widow to a suffering narcissist.

At the time, I was working in Connecticut while my brother Mark, recently released from prison, was staying with Mom. I tried to help by putting her on my insurance and paying her bills. As I prepared to call her, I reflected on my need to stay connected to someone who had treated me so badly.

When I finally called, Mom asked when I was coming home. "Mom, I live in Connecticut now but have some news to share." The silence on the other end made me nervous, but I pressed on. "I've been accepted to the University of London. I'm moving to the UK next September. That gives you almost a year to adjust."

After a long pause, she finally spoke. "I'll be dead long before then," and hung up. I stood there, holding the buzzing phone.

On December 24th, Mark called to tell me that Mom had

been taken to the hospital. He had found her passed out on the floor with a distended stomach. On Christmas Day, I called her at the hospital in Pittsburgh. "I want to go home," she sobbed.

"Don't you want the doctors to find out what happened?" I asked.

"I hate it here! It smells!" she cried like a child. I gave in.

"They can't keep you if you don't want to stay. Call Mark and ask him to bring you home."

Mom signed a release, and Mark took her home. Over the next two months, I prepared for my move to London. I sold my condo and planned to stay with Cheryl, a client-turned-friend, before leaving. I requested and received a leave of absence from work at AT&T, knowing I'd never return to the corporate grind. Then, in April, Mark called again.

"Mom's in the hospital. You better come quick." My heart sank. I packed a bag and drove to Pittsburgh.

At Allegheny General Hospital, I found Mom waiting on a gurney outside a testing lab, her abdomen distended. "What did the doctor say?" I asked.

"They're running tests," she said, touching her swollen belly. "They drained me last night, and now it's worse." She closed her eyes, and I waited with her.

Mom was diagnosed with pancreatic cancer that had spread everywhere. When she fell into a coma, her sisters, Stella and Martha, visited. Stella blamed me. "This is your fault," she said.

"How do you figure?" I asked, holding back my fury.

"You should have stayed home to take care of her after your father died. Your selfishness is killing her." Furious, I left the hospital.

Mom died four weeks later, never waking from her coma. Instead of attending her funeral, I went to California for a metaphysical workshop and cried most of the trip. Mom had predicted she'd die before I moved to London. I canceled my plans, telling myself that moving wouldn't change my life. Wherever I went, my issues would follow. I focused on my life and healing instead. Years later, I realized I had missed a great opportunity. The inheritance from Mom could have covered my living expenses, but I chose a familiar path of misery.

Looking back, I realized that I blamed myself for Mom's death and used guilt to punish myself for years. I discovered what I call the Boomerang Effect: instead of ending toxic relationships with my family, I kept going back for more. Mom's death was a missed opportunity for growth. Over time, I forgave myself and my family and focused on building my life as a writer.

Plot Points

To Recap:

- Seeing crisis as an opportunity can be a powerful mindset that helps us navigate challenging times and emerge stronger.
- Instead of ignoring the challenges or minimizing the impact of the crisis, consider acknowledging the potential for positive change that can be found within the difficulty.
- Fear of the unknown and uncertainty are important feelings to acknowledge when change happens.

What's Your Story?

Addressing obstacles and challenges is a twofold process. Often, experiences from our past hold an energetic connection to the present, as was the case with my mom's death. This connection is especially true for unresolved trauma and triggering events. These triggers highlight areas that need attention for greater happiness and freedom.

Unresolved crises tend to repeat themselves. The first step in breaking this cycle is to think back and identify historical challenges. This might involve recalling memories, asking friends or family members for their perspectives, or seeking help from a therapist or coach.

Once you've discovered the original obstacle, continue the process outlined below.

Step 1: Revisit the Original Crisis

Start by examining the original crisis that created the trauma, viewing it from a new perspective. In an earlier chapter story, I recalled sitting in the office after the fight at school, waiting for the consequences. What I didn't share was that Jennifer's father stormed in while we were sitting there and slapped her hard across the face. I felt sorry for her and the difficult home life she must have had. This made me feel compassion for Jennifer and work on forgiving her and the others involved.

Many of the people who harassed me did so as part of a group, with Donna Delveccio as the ringleader. She disliked me in grade school and used junior high to make my life miserable, leveraging her leadership to rally others against me. As an adult, I realized that many kids joined her out of fear of becoming targets themselves.

Step 2: Assess the Severity

Start by determining the severity of the crisis or challenge. Then, identify what you can control. In cases of severe loss, such as a divorce or the death of a loved one, the best course of action is often to allow yourself to grieve. Grieving is a vital part of the healing process and cannot be rushed. Honor your grief as a reminder of the importance of the person or relationship. Creating a dedicated space with tokens of the lost person or relationship can help you remember the good times. Seeking support from friends, family, or support groups is also essential.

Step 3: Control Your Attitude

In less severe crises, focus on what you can control, like your attitude. For example, when facing work deadlines, distractions can increase stress. Break the pattern by taking a walk outside or changing your environment. This helps you return to the present moment, where you can be more effective.

Similarly, if you don't get a job you interviewed for, view it as an opportunity for something better. After I missed the chance to study in London, I applied to The American Film Institute in Los Angeles, which turned out to be one of the best decisions of my life.

Step 4: Shift Your Perspective

Look at the situation from another angle. This concept was explored in the chapter on "Point of View." In this case, try to understand the perspectives of others involved. Recognizing that my bullies had their own personal pain helped me see beyond my victimhood. Can you view your challenge from a different perspective and see yourself as a catalyst for change rather than a victim?

Step 5: Find the Opportunity

Consider the challenge as a learning opportunity rather than an obstacle. This mindset allows you to work with the experience rather than battle against it. Fighting the challenge often prolongs the situation and increases misery. Instead, ask yourself if there's something to learn or a new direction to explore. This can lead to personal growth.

Step 6: Seek External Support

A fresh pair of eyes can reveal hidden opportunities. Therapists and coaches are excellent resources, but trusted friends or family members can also offer valuable insights. The key is to open to new perspectives and approaches through whatever obstacle arises. Life is full of ups and downs, and developing the skills to navigate them is crucial for a well-lived life.

10

Turning the Page

Everything is possible, even the impossible.

— Mary Poppins, *Mary Poppins Returns*

January 1986

AT&T transferred me to Connecticut to work on the Cigna Insurance account. I needed to get out of Washington, DC, after I'd made a mess of all my relationships, leaving me friendless and loveless. When my boss approached me about the work in Connecticut, I jumped at the chance, hoping this would give me the new start I so desperately wanted after Dad had died and left me angry, lost, and hopeless.

It was about the same time I realized that Dad's death sent me into an even deeper spiral and showed me just how bad my life was. If I didn't figure something out soon, I was doomed to a life of misery and unhappiness. Connecticut might be just what I needed. AT&T paid my moving expenses and gave me a bonus that allowed me to buy a two-bedroom condo. I kept to myself and didn't look to do much socially until I felt better about myself. My work as an account executive meant that I spent most of my time at my client's offices in Windsor and Bloomfield. There, I met Margo and Cheryl, who were employees of Cigna, although in different departments. Margo was ten years older than me and had a horse that she loved to talk about. Cheryl was closer in age and was into metaphysics. Cheryl tried to get me to go and see psychics and have my horoscope read. I wasn't into it, so I called it "Woo Woo," and thought Cheryl was stranger than most people I was typically drawn to.

Both Margo and Cheryl seemed uninterested in men, which meant I wouldn't try to snag anyone they were dating. Most importantly, while Cheryl occasionally had a glass of wine, Margo never drank anything but coffee and sparkling water. I decided to give up my drinking habits, which meant no more bars and no more cases of beer to stock my fridge.

One day at lunch, Cheryl said, "There's an event at the metaphysical shop in Glastonbury. I want you to go with me. I know you hate the idea, but I just want you to try it this once. If you do, I promise I won't bother you again."

I thought about my empty fridge and said, "If we can grab some dinner, I'll go. But don't make me promise anything."

Cheryl was thrilled and said, "Just try to keep an open mind."

I grunted. We made plans to meet after work and drive together.

At 5:15, I pulled up to the curb outside Cheryl's building in Windsor. I waited a few minutes until Cheryl rushed out and got in the car. "Nice car. Very clean!" Cheryl said as she got in, sat, and put on her seat belt.

I laughed. My Toyota Corolla was almost a year old and had survived its first harsh winter well. We made small talk as we drove and finally arrived at the Somerset Shoppes. Cheryl led me to the Ways of the Winds store. I laughed to myself and wondered why metaphysical stores had such strange names.

The shop was filled with crystals of every shape and size, which intrigued me. It reminded me of how I collected rocks since I was a child, finding one on the road or sidewalk or in the trees behind my family's house. I cherished the rocks and kept them with me wherever I went. But I'd never seen anything like the store's huge, polished crystal ball that felt soft to the touch. There was rose quartz carved and raw, amethyst, onyx, and many others I didn't know. I let myself get lost in the rocks while soft music played and the smell of something lovely and not overly perfumed filled the air. Unaware of how much time had passed, I was brought out of my reverie when Cheryl approached. "Come on—they're starting."

I asked, "Who's starting what?"

"Just come on. Remember. Open mind." Cheryl walked me to the back of the store where chairs were set up in front of a riser with one chair. The only seats available were two in the front. We sat; the room quieted. I wanted to say something, but it was too late. A large woman in flowing robes, her white hair pulled back in a smooth ponytail, walked in and took the seat on the riser. The woman wore large rings of different stones, some of which I recognized. She wore long earrings and a yellow stone necklace that fell onto her lap. She looked around the room and smiled. Her voice was soft but powerful as she spoke, "Welcome, dear ones. It's wonderful to see so many familiar faces and a couple of new ones."

I cringed when the woman looked at me. Was I that different from anyone here?

The woman continued. "Tonight, I am channeling The Collective. The Collective, for those who are new (another look towards me), is a multidimensional group of entities that speak through me and bring messages of hope and peace to the world. They'll start with a brief chat and then will ask for questions. For now, I'm going into a trance. See you on the other side!" The woman closed her eyes and took three deep inhales and long exhales. I looked around at all the faces filled with excitement and wonder and thought, "Yep. A Cult."

Suddenly, a voice boomed near me. "Welcome, welcome, welcome!" The voice belonged to the woman, only it was high-pitched, loud, and pithy. The woman/Collective spoke of the coming age and how the world would evolve. How beings and entities from places we would never believe were watching us here in this time space, cheering us on from afar. We were loved and we would have to stay focused on Love to get through to the new age. After some time, The Collective stopped what I would call a monologue of hooey, and the woman spread her arms. "Now to you here. Who has a question?"

Everyone raised their hands. Everyone except me, who only wanted to hide under my chair. Someone was selected and asked their question, which sounded mundane—about a boyfriend and whether he would ever ask her to marry him—after the big lead-in of huge evolutionary shifts in the cosmos. After a couple more, the woman/Collective asked for one last question. Cheryl nearly jumped out of her chair. The woman/Collective smiled and said, "Yes, we see you! What is your question?"

Cheryl had her question ready. "I'm here with a new friend that I feel such a strong connection with. I feel like she is my sister. Can you tell me anything about that?"

I was mortified. My face felt either blistering red or white hot. I stared straight ahead, not daring to make eye contact with the woman/Collective. I wanted to jump and get out of there, but that would only mean that everyone knew it was me who Cheryl spoke of. But would they? How did anyone know we came together? So, we sat down at the same time, but that's only because these were the last two seats. I clamped my jaw shut, fearing I'd scream out.

"What an interesting question! Well, of course we feel the connection with you both. In our seeing, you were sisters in this very area, maybe further north and east, nearer say what you now call "Boston." You were close, as close as sisters can be. You worked magic together, quietly of course because these were times of great danger for women with your gifts. But you worked your magic and changed realities for those that knew you and came to you, always keeping your secret. It was a beautiful time for you both. And now you've returned to be together again in this time of the new age. There is magic to work together, you and this friend. May it be wondrous for you both." After that, the woman/Collective said their farewells. The woman nodded, opened her eyes and smiled.

The evening ended, I jumped from my seat and walked as fast as I could to the exit. The cold air felt fresh on my burning face and cooled my churning heart. I paced until Cheryl finally made it out of the door carrying a bag. She walked up to me and before I could say anything, handed me the bag.

"I think you'll like this."

I accepted the bag, looked inside, and found a book, The Sacred Journey, written by someone called Lazaris. I didn't want to seem ungrateful. I'd been thinking of what I'd say to Cheryl. Cheryl was, after all, my client, who had shared something very strange with me, making me question what I was doing here in Connecticut hanging out with the weirdest person I'd ever met. And now this book. I stared at the cover while getting my thoughts in order.

"Interesting. Thanks, Cheryl, and thanks for the unusual evening."

Cheryl didn't seem to notice the fear, worry, or doubt in my voice. The entire drive back, she discussed every detail that the Collective brought up and luckily didn't let me respond even to the questions she asked. I was relieved to finally drop Cheryl off at her car and drive away, wondering what had just happened.

A few weeks passed before I picked up the book again. Cheryl had asked me about it a couple of times during lunch, but I put her off, saying that I was taking my time to let it all in. One morning, I woke over an hour early. I ate breakfast and dressed for work in record time. With some time to go before leaving for the office, I looked for something to do that would be more enjoyable than sitting in traffic. Scanning the room, my eyes landed on the book from Cheryl, The Sacred Journey. Reading a chapter wouldn't hurt; at least, I can say I read it.

I sat down and started reading. An hour later, I checked the time and saw that it was almost time to leave. Instead, I picked up the phone and called my office. "Hi, Melissa. It's Carrie. I'm not coming into the office today. I'm not feeling well. Yes, I'll see you tomorrow."

That done, I continued reading and finished the 150-page book before 2:00 p.m. I grabbed my coat and went to my car. I drove to the Somerset Shoppes in Glastonbury and walked to the Ways of the Winds store. The shop had only a couple of customers. Holding the book, I walked directly to the counter and said, "What other books do you have by this Lazaris guy?"

The woman looked at me and said in precise tones, "La-ZAR-us."

I replied, "Okay laZARus. Where are the books?"

"That's the only book so far, but you're in luck. They're doing a workshop in Philadelphia this weekend and we're sending a van. There's a couple of seats left if you want to go."

Surprising myself, I didn't hesitate. "Yes. Sign me up."

"Will your friend from the other night be joining you?"

Now I was really torn. Cheryl was a client who had brought me here in the first place, and now to spend a weekend with her? I turned to the woman and said, "Hold a seat for her, too, and I will call you once I confirm." I worked with the woman to get the tickets and a hotel room and left.

Later that day, I confirmed that Cheryl would go.

I had no idea that my life was about to take a most unusual turn in a way that changed me forever.

UNDERSTANDING YOUR MOTIVATION

Anyone and everything can change. Rewriting your story is a powerful way to create a new life experience. When you shift your script, the story transforms, and the characters around you respond to the new narrative. But how do you achieve this change, and how do you make it stick? It all starts with understanding why you want to change.

Why do you want to shift? I discussed motivation in an earlier chapter. It's now time to apply it to your new story.

Your motivation might stem from a significant life event, such as marriage, the birth of a child, or a major transition like a divorce or children leaving home. My reason was intense emotional and psychological pain, signaling that I was on a path of self-destruction if I stayed where I was. Moving to Connecticut was exactly what I needed to rewrite my story. When AT&T offered me the move, I initially thought I was running away and almost turned it down. But recognizing the mess I had made of my life in Virginia, I accepted the offer. Disrupting the repetitive story I was living was a crucial motivation.

WHY CHANGE YOUR NARRATIVE?

Realizing why you want a new life motivates you to embrace and focus on your updated theme and story. Here are a few reasons to change your personal narrative:

1. **Break Free from Limiting Beliefs**: Your life story is often shaped by your upbringing, experiences, and societal views. Changing your narrative allows you to break free from limiting beliefs and live authentically, embracing your true desires and values.

2. **Unlock Your Potential**: The initial story often underestimates your capabilities. Rewriting your story opens you up

to your potential, allowing you to pursue a happier, more fulfilling life and embrace new experiences and opportunities.

3. **Learn from Your Mistakes**: Everyone makes mistakes. Changing your narrative allows you to learn from these mistakes, forgive yourself, and move forward positively. This helps build self-esteem and a stronger sense of self-worth.

4. **Adapt to Change**: Life throws curveballs. A new story enhances your ability to adapt to challenges and opportunities. As your values and priorities change, a new story allows you to evolve with an expanding worldview. It also helps you stay relevant, embrace new skills, and adapt to a constantly changing reality.

MY JOURNEY OF CHANGE

One of my stories centered around the trauma I endured in my infancy. Living in constant fear, not knowing when I'd be fed or cared for, affected my beliefs about myself and life's possibilities. My focus on survival lasted well into my twenties. It wasn't until I read *The Sacred Journey* that I considered another way of existing. This book helped me turn the page and begin rewriting my story, shifting my focus to healing and new perspectives.

THE PLOT THICKENS

Knowing why you want to rewrite your story leads to the next question: how? In each chapter, I've described steps to discover the story elements. It's time to incorporate all those elements into a new narrative about your life.

EMBRACING THE POWER OF LIFE STORIES

Before discovering the power of life stories, I followed the clues life sent me. In the story above, it started with a book Cheryl gave me. Cheryl and I attended a Lazaris event in Philadelphia, which opened my eyes to the possibility of living a happier life. The idea of freedom resonated with me. Although I wasn't deeply involved in personal development, working with the Lazaris materials was a great start. Lazaris talked about the process of change, which made sense to me. If I wanted lasting improvements, the work needed to address my complexities while being simple enough to keep my interest. Below, I've shared the steps of the Lazaris process that took me on a deep journey of discovery.

STEPS TO CHANGE: RECOGNIZE, ACKNOWLEDGE, FORGIVE, AND CHANGE

Step 1: Recognize

Change begins with awareness. Identify the quality, habit, or way of being—the story—that no longer works for you. Instead of vaguely wanting to stop feeling sad, focus on specific habits. For example, you might say, "I have a habit of feeling bad about myself when I make a mistake. I tell myself that I am stupid." Recognize this as part of your story where you are always the sad or unhappy protagonist.

Step 2: Acknowledge

Own your actions and thoughts. Acknowledging that they are yours, empowers you to change them. Without ownership, you can't do anything about them. Acknowledge the emotions, sadness, and pain you experience when you make a mistake. Consider why you feel that making a mistake is terrible. Having done the work earlier to understand your story's theme, plot, and characters is crucial for this step. Acknowledge how everything is woven into your narrative. This allows you to shift more easily.

Step 3: Forgive

Let go of judgments, resentments, anger, grudges, bitterness, and pain. Forgiveness is about understanding why someone did what they did. If you can't forgive the action, forgive the reason behind it. I learned to forgive my mother because she was damaged by her own family's story and suffered from mental health problems. Understanding her issues helped me let go of my bitterness, lifting a weight off my shoulders. Forgiveness is a conscious decision that sets you free.

Step 4: Change

Forgiveness doesn't mean forgetting. It's about acknowledging the pain and opting to respond differently. It's about learning from the experience and being wiser. Forgiveness allows you to thrive and grow by letting go of the emotions around the pain. Acknowledge the hurt, see it, and move on; accepting the outcome and living a happy and fulfilling life. You can't change others or undo mistakes, but you can change how you respond to situations.

THE IMPORTANCE OF SELF-FORGIVENESS

Self-forgiveness is just as important. When you hurt someone, you might feel terrible afterward. You can apologize, but sometimes the damage is irreparable. You need to forgive yourself for being human and making mistakes. Understand why you acted the way you did. Were you angry, hurt, or projecting your shame onto someone else? You can't forgive yourself until you see the why and feel remorse. Once you do, forgive yourself and change. Feel the emotions, ask for help from a coach, therapist of trusted friend, and move forward.

THE FORGIVENESS PROCESS

a. Acknowledge What You Are Forgiving

Write down what you are forgiving in a journal or document. This helps you connect with your feelings. For example, forgiving my parents had multiple layers. Initially, I tried blanket forgiveness for my early years and had some success. However, I found greater success by addressing key situations, such as my mother not feeding me. Once I understood the event or situation, I gained perspective by putting myself in her shoes.

b. Meditative Process for Forgiveness

Sit quietly and close your eyes. Imagine yourself in a beautiful meadow with a massive tree under a gorgeous sunny sky. Walk to the tree and sit with your back against its trunk, feeling its strength. Then, visualize someone you need to forgive standing on the other side of the tree. Face this person and stand tall. Tell them how they wronged you and how it felt. Express your anger, hurt, and pain. Take as long as you need, but go for it, telling the person everything you've been holding back. When you feel complete, ask the person, "Why? Why did you do this to me?" Listen patiently for their response, which may reveal their own pain, hurt, sorrow, or shame that had nothing to do with you. This understanding can help release the hurtful act that you've held onto.

c. Express Forgiveness

Tell them you forgive them. Observe their reaction as they accept your forgiveness.

You may want to do this meditation a couple of times to feel the impact of forgiving someone. Trust that you will know when you've forgiven.

MAKING THE DECISION TO CHANGE

Changing your story is a personal decision. By understanding the potential benefits, you can make an informed choice about the new narrative you want to write. Embrace the journey of self-discovery and remember that the process involves continuous reflection and growth. Stay aware, practice forgiveness, and seek support when needed. With dedication, you can transform your story into one of resilience, empowerment, and fulfillment.

Plot Points

To Recap:

- It is possible to change any story in your life. It starts with knowing why you're ready to tell a new story.
- Start by recognizing the story you want to change and accepting that it's your story; you wrote it, and you can rewrite it.
- The most important step is forgiveness.

What's Your Story?

You've decided to turn the page and write a new story. Here are the steps to support you in your journey:

Step 1: Recognize the Story You Want to Change

Identify the story that you want to change. Write about it in your journal in as much detail as feels right. You might start with a relationship story or something to do with work or finances. You might also have a health story that's causing concern. It's important to choose one for now. You can add others as you get comfortable with the process.

Step 2: Acknowledge Ownership

Accept that it's your story. You wrote it. This may be uncomfortable, but it is also empowering—when you claim responsibility for writing it, you can rewrite it.

Step 3: Forgive

Forgive the characters and yourself for the roles played in your narrative.

Step 4: Feel Compassion

Feel the compassion that comes from understanding. Compassion is a powerful force that helps facilitate change.

Example from My Personal Experience

When I first discovered the pain and shame my mother lived with and the abuse she endured as a child, I felt sorry for her. But I wondered why she took it out on me. Especially as I started my journey to rewrite my story, I experienced rage and pain that my mom didn't love me enough to take action and become a better person. This brought up old feelings of inadequacy. If this happens to you, don't dwell on these negative thoughts—they serve no purpose and can re-traumatize you. Instead, focus on the goodness of your current life. This process constantly reminded me to stay present and remember all the great things I've become, especially as a woman who broke the cycle that defined her story. When I reached that point, I found compassion and forgave my mother again. I saw her as a person before she became a mother, a little girl mistreated by her family. I cried for her and for the person she wanted to be but couldn't become. That's compassion: understanding and concern for the challenges others face.

Step 5: Embrace Change

Pay attention to your thoughts and actions. Observe when you're about to follow an old pattern and consciously choose to change.

By following these steps, you can effectively rewrite your story, moving towards a life of empowerment and fulfillment.

And in the end...

All we have to do is decide what to do with the time that is given us.

— Gandalf, *The Lord of the Rings*

July 2012

I sat in the old steam train that traveled from Buckfast to Totnes, a market town at the head of the estuary of the River Dart in Devon. I loved the train. It reminded me of the charm of my beloved England. I was on my way to meet Simon for coffee. I thought about the first time I had met him in Washington, DC. He walked into a meeting where they introduced me as the new project lead. It turned out Simon was there on behalf of the new board of directors. They went around the room making introductions. When Simon spoke, his smooth British accent caught my attention. But after the meeting, he was formal and stuffy when I went to speak to him. I was disappointed that he had the personality of a toad. Over time, Simon opened up and showed an occasional playful side featuring his dry British wit. While I loved the humor, I found him difficult to get to know beyond the project we were on.

After the project ended and I returned to Los Angeles, Simon and I stayed in contact. It was fun discovering that he was writing a thriller, so I sent him a book I was developing. With our back-and-forth over a shared love of writing, we became friends. And now I was on my way to meet him in Totnes.

The train arrived. I started my climb up High Street, passing Cornwall pasty shops, bookstores, and restaurants preparing scones for afternoon tea. I loved being in England. I thought about my choice to spend the summer at my friend Rowan's cottage. It was a dream come true. So much so that I considered extending my stay beyond my scheduled October return. It meant I'd have to find a paying gig; my savings were running low. But for now, I was looking forward to seeing Simon. I had to admit that I was a little lonely, isolated at Natsworthy Cottage far away from everything and without a car.

I arrived at the pub and saw Simon sitting outside at a table. He saw me and smiled. I walked over to him and took a seat. "I hope you weren't waiting long."

"My mother lives around the corner. I was walking around and decided to grab the table when I saw it was open."

I asked. "Your mother lives in Totnes?"

"I'm from Totnes. The Arcturus Book Shop was my home when I was in school."

That shocked me even more. The Arcturus Book Shop was the first place Rowan had taken me to when I first arrived at Natsworthy Cottage. Simon and I talked a bit longer, mostly small talk, when Simon said, "I've been invited to dinner at a friend's home and thought you might want to go. I'll take you back to your cottage after."

I thought meeting more people and feeling less isolated would be nice. We bought a bottle of wine and walked up a side lane towards his friend's home. Their place was warm and inviting, filled with the aroma of roast pork. Jim and Katie welcomed me, asking too many questions. I started to wonder what Simon had told them. I decided to go full American on them. "Am I being interviewed?"

Simon pursed his lips, but I thought it was more to hide a smile than anything. Jim, after a few glasses of wine, said, "American through and through!" Katie grabbed his arm and tried to stop him, but to no avail.

"Simon hasn't brought anyone around for decades. We were slightly surprised when he said he was bringing a friend." I put it aside but did wonder if there was more to this meeting than I thought.

Shortly after, we left and walked to Simon's car for the drive to Natsworthy, chatting along the way. I learned that Simon was a serious musician and that his divorce had been finalized a year before. I knew he was separated and wondered if his divorce contributed to his new openness.

We arrived at the cottage, and Simon asked to come in and get a coffee for the drive back. We talked about Simon's ex-wife, his son, and their lives. He was more open now, and I wondered if he'd had more to drink than I thought. We talked about our dreams and my passion for England. But it was getting late, and I worried about him driving back to Totnes.

Finally, Simon was ready to go. He hugged me, and when I thought he'd kiss my cheek, he reached in and kissed me deeply on the lips. I was shocked and repeated in my mind, "Just relax and enjoy. It's okay." When the kiss ended, I looked at him. He said, "I think I've been in love with you for some time now. I think it happened after your last trip to Washington."

I thought back to when I was in DC. Simon was there for meetings, and we met for lunch at a great Thai restaurant we loved. I didn't know that there was anything more than friendship between us. I recovered from his words and said, "How could you know that? We've never even been on a date."

Simon looked at me and smiled. "What are you doing for dinner tomorrow? I know a great pub in Lustley."

Later that night, I had trouble falling asleep. Simon snored softly beside me. I kept thinking I was dreaming. At 55, it felt like I was in my first relationship. It scared the shit out of me for more than one reason. I'd never dated anyone for more than a couple of weeks, and, for some reason, this felt incredibly real. More importantly, I knew beyond any doubt that rewriting my stories worked. Living in England and now the possibility of being in a relationship with a great guy meant that dream endings can happen. It was time to write another chapter.

WRITING NEW STORIES

When you rewrite a story, you acknowledge the ending of one story, one dream, so that another can begin. After years of working on my Life As a Story, I've experienced this more than once and expect the stories I'm in now will conclude at their best time with another one already written and waiting in the wings. The story above shows the start of my relationship with Simon. That was twelve years ago as of this writing. Since then, I've changed my story around my work and the places I want to live. Simon and I share some stories, and we each have our own. It's a perfect situation for me, and one I noted in one of my many journals when I wrote that I wanted a truly committed partnership. It was perfectly aligned with living in England—another important dream. Stories flow from one to another; they are cumulative and can add to each earlier story. You might even want to look at them as sequels with new characters and new themes and plots.

As you begin reviewing and rewriting your stories, you'll notice that they are integral to who you are. As such, you can take charge of the themes and plots to improve them. Improving your stories brings happiness and fulfillment in ways that you might not have expected.

Your stories are revised for any number of reasons. Some of the things I've written about include life changes like marriage or children. Sometimes, the ending is the natural conclusion of the story, the third act where the heroine reaches her goal. Sometimes, it's when you recognize that the story you're in isn't working, and it's time to take a new approach. In my work, I encourage people to look at their stories and see where they can change the parts that no longer serve them. Ultimately, the idea is to seek the best life you can make for yourself, find a dream, a purpose, and go after it. As someone who lived this kind of transformation, I know it's possible, and as a life story coach, I've helped others reach for and live extraordinary lives.

THE PLOT THICKENS

April 2022

I was frustrated. After all my work with my stories, I found myself back doing the work I had hoped to walk away from. I wanted to blame the pandemic and the mess it made of so many lives. But, at this stage of my life, I knew that blame indicated that I needed to go inside and find the theme and ending of this story I was in. After all, it is an inside job.

Our friends Louisa and Peter had invited Simon and me to dinner. Louisa was a violinist, and Peter played the French Horn. Simon played classical bassoon. They all connected through the music they loved. Louisa and Peter saw me as a great agent of change; any time I was with them, I felt at ease.

After a wonderful dinner of homemade pasta and delicious Chianti, Louisa took me aside. "Have you recovered from all this pandemic craziness?"

I smirked, which is something that many do when the topic of the pandemic comes up. "It depends on what you mean. I've had to go back to some of my old clients to bring in money since I lost work and haven't recovered yet. I'm still building my coaching business, and my income isn't what I want it to be, so there you have it."

Louisa laughed. "I might have to call bullshit on that, Carrie. You're brilliant, and you've helped so many. Why don't you give a Ted Talk or, better, write a book? Do something to get your message out there. You know you have our love and support."

I thanked her and honestly wanted to discount Louisa's words, but they stuck with me. When we returned home, I went to my office and opened my journal. I looked at my career story and realized I was back in survival mode. The pandemic had done that to me. When I realized where I was and the story I was living, I first forgave myself. I was human, and falling back into an old pattern made sense, especially with something that shook up the world and the psyche of everyone on the planet.

Next, I opened to a blank page and wrote, "I am an Ordinary Person."

This story shows how, at any time, life can throw you a curve ball. I was old enough to know that the world would somehow get through the pandemic, but on a personal level, I was a mess. At times like these, I knew that looking at the stories I was living was the fastest way to write a new, happier chapter. With this realization, I decided to focus my energy on creating the business I wanted, helping people see the value of life stories, and authoring an easy and successful life.

I worked on my new story and took the following steps:

Gratitude acknowledges the gifts in life, opening you to even more blessings. I felt deep gratitude for Louisa and her willingness to tell me what I needed to hear. Few friends have the courage to speak the truth, and Louisa was special in this regard.

Grief can be useful when moving on from an old way of being. It's easy to ignore the grieving process, especially if you believe grief is only for losing a loved one. However, grief is about any loss, including the loss of an old way of life. Embracing grief allows you to fully process changes and move forward.

Make **forgiveness** a daily practice. I discuss forgiveness in detail in the previous chapter "Turning the Page." Everyone makes mistakes or does things they're not proud of. By practicing daily forgiveness, you free yourself from judgments and negative thoughts that can undermine your sense of empowerment.

Recognize the **continuity** of your life story. Your stories are interconnected, and rewriting one can impact others, leading to even more compelling narratives. As I moved through this process, I saw how everything was connected, from the issues with my mother and home life to where I am today.

Plot Points

May 2024

The midday sun filled the dining room at the home I shared with Simon in Santa Barbara. I sat at the beautiful wooden table Simon had hired a craftsman to build many years ago. I rubbed my hand across the top, admiring the workmanship as I'd done so many times. On the other side of the table, a man pulled a stack of documents, a pouch, and several pens out of his bag.

I watched him and felt my nerves start to fray. I thought about how my emotions went everywhere these last few weeks, from joy to sadness and excitement. The condo in the Century City area of Los Angeles was a dream come true. Seventeen years ago, I'd made enough for a down payment and purchased the unit. It was just as the housing market was starting to fall. The condo was smaller than I'd hoped and needed an upgrade, but the price was right, and the remodel idea was intriguing. That was important to me. I envisioned buying a place in disrepair, fixing it, and renting it out. I had had the dream for so many years I wondered if it would ever happen. But then I started working on my stories, and I started to change.

I was happy to live in the condo, especially since the space was ideal. It was on the fourteenth floor with stunning views of the mountains, the Hollywood sign, and downtown Los Angeles miles away. At night, I'd watch the planes coming into LAX. Their lights filled the starless night in stunning alignment as they waited for their time to touch down. On the nights of a full moon, the sky was filled with a huge lunar sphere.

I loved the place, and when I got the project in Washington, DC, I had the money to remodel and be out of town while it was under construction. I used the building homeowner's association staff to help oversee the work. In six months, the remodel was complete. The updated space was lovely and admired by everyone. I was proud of my efforts and advertised it for rent. The timing was perfect. Shortly after I secured my first tenant, Simon and I started our relationship, so I moved in with him in Pennsylvania before we both came back to Southern California.

Now, after all these years, I was preparing to sign the papers, selling the Century City condo. It was the ending of one dream and starting another in Santa Barbara with Simon. The notary from the escrow company gave me page after page to sign. I'd had tenants for the last twelve years and was grateful for everything I'd learned and experienced with this dream come true. My expenses were covered, and except for one bad tenant, ***I*** *was very happy with the experience. All the ups and downs gave me something I'd never had before: insights into myself and the person I'd become. It was time to let this story go and write the next chapter. The tears would come later.*

◇◇

I could not think of a better way to end this book except with a story of endings and beginnings—and magic. I wrote the story above when I first put my Century City condo on the market in December 2023. It marked the end of a dream I'd had—to own, remodel, and rent out the property. I knew how important this dream was, so the ending had to be meaningful. The interesting part? I closed on the sale of the condo on May 29, 2024. When I reached that chapter during one of the book's rewrites, I paused. Each chapter includes a date stamp of the story I share. At the time, I had no idea when I'd actually sell the condo so I selected the date, "May 2024" without realizing how close it would come to reality. It was a beautiful reminder that when we let life flow, our dreams can fall into place.

What's Your Story?

When someone asks, "That story ended; what now?" My answer is simple: Write the next chapter. Here are a few things to keep in mind as you rewrite your story:

Step 1: Visualize the Ending

Have a clear idea of how you want your story to end. Take the example of me selling my condo. When I first wrote the date, it was, at the time, a random idea of how long it would take to get a buyer and then close on the deal. Interestingly, I got the offer in early May. The buyer was very motivated and wanted to close in two weeks. Somehow, it all fell into place, making my initial thought of "May 2024" a reality.

So, while living your current story, envision the desired outcome. I've used journaling to explore various ideas and dreams, helping me process what I imagine my life to be. For example, I imagined how freeing it would be to no longer own my condo in Los Angeles. The thought of being free from the mortgage, HOA fees, and taxes was liberating. Not having to worry about tenants meant more energy for my future dreams, and the potential financial gain from the sale was also exciting.

My shelves are filled with journals I've kept over the years. Looking through them, I'm often amazed at how many dreams have come true—perhaps not exactly as I wrote them, but mostly better than I had imagined.

Step 2: Cultivate Gratitude

Feel gratitude for the new story you're writing. Think about the amazing adventure ahead. Gratitude is powerful and attracts more things for which to be grateful. I worked with a woman who hated her job and constantly complained. She wasn't getting any responses to her job applications. I suggested she find three things she was grateful for about her job and write them down daily. She started with the income and the friends she'd made. Within three weeks, she had several job offers. Gratitude shifted her perspective and expanded her opportunities.

Step 3: Embrace Challenges

When challenges arise, see them as opportunities to respond differently. They are chances to recognize your growth and demonstrate your courage, resilience, or determination. Congratulate yourself on your progress and keep moving forward.

Step 4: It's an Inside Job.

Take responsibility for your old story—its themes, characters, plot, and point of view. Recognize that you shaped and spun everything that has happened in your life. By owning your story, you gain the power to change it all.

Step 5: Build a Support System

Have a coach, therapist, trusted friend, or family member to confide in. A support system helps you break old stories and stay focused on your new narrative.

Step 6: Connect with Your Future Self

Visualize your Future Self living the new story. In a quiet, meditative state, close your eyes and imagine this future you. You don't need to know how far into the future they exist; just know that there is a future that is calling you. See them in a room or in nature, whatever feels right for you. In this future, you are sitting in a chair or next to a tree; be open and have fun with whatever shows up. Go to them where they are sitting and just be there. You don't need to say anything; know that the new story is already written, and this future self is proof of that.

Step 7: Stay Aware and Practice

Keep a journal to track the shifts you notice in your life. Over time, these changes will become more apparent, and your reality will transform.

Epilogue

To those who have faced emotional and psychological trauma, to those who have felt the need to shrink themselves and hide their true, authentic selves just to survive—I see you. Life can make us feel small, but it doesn't have to define us. That story doesn't have to be your ending.

Through the steps in *Life Rewritten*, you've explored the incredible power of stories—not just to understand where you've been but to reshape where you're going. Storytelling offers the clarity to see the patterns of the past, the forgiveness to release the pain, and the gratitude to embrace the present. With these tools, you can step boldly into the life you were always meant to live.

The pen is in your hand. You have the strength to rewrite anything that no longer serves you. This book is your guide, but the journey is yours. Your new story begins now. Let it be one filled with hope, courage, and the joy of living authentically.

I wish you all the success you truly deserve.

For additional help, PDF downloads, resources and information on scheduling a private session, visit my website, carriekcwest.com, where you will find more ideas and support. For your convenience, please use the QR Code below:

Acknowledgements

As a writer, I always thought the hardest part of finishing a book was staring at the blank page. Turns out, I was wrong. The real challenge begins after you hit "save." Getting a book ready for publication takes a great many people. I've been incredibly fortunate to have an amazing group of people by my side. It's with deep gratitude and love that I acknowledge everyone who has been part of this journey. Thank you for making this dream a reality.

Simon Knight – my partner in all parts of life. Your support is everything.

Thelma Alane – my sister and lifelong friend. We made it.

Sue Kiel – my mentor and friend who left us way too soon.

Zoe Landers – my dear friend and fellow magician

And to this amazing cast of characters whose love and support sustained me throughout the process: Barne Kiel, Grif Griffis, Dan Knight, Remy Landon. Rahla Kahn, Richard Rossner, Jenn Brown, Lisa Dale Norton, Susan Crossman, Kelly Pasholk, Peggy Fitzsimmons, John Lavack, Carole Reed, Julie Cassinelli, Tiffany Rochelle, Katrina Fernandez, Rebecca Marder, Nancy Mathison, Jeff Lyons, Lisa Segal, Lazaris and Concept: Synergy, Beverly Kittaen-Morse and IBP, Charmaine Hammond, Victoria Bennett, Nancy Gordon, Nelson Scott, Debora Hollick, Lilian Sue, Gloria Treister, Brian Werdesheim, Savannah Pincus, Lori Leyden, Andrew Johnstone, Alisonn Rose, Mary West, Diana Benzaquen, Ken and Lauren Berris, Tracey Becker, Tom Harris, Melissa Converse, Cassi Flynn.

About the Author

Carrie KC West has spent her life immersed in the transformative power of stories. Her journey began long before earning a Master of Fine Arts in filmmaking from the prestigious American Film Institute, where she spent two intensive years honing the craft of storytelling. As a script and book reader for production companies, she dissected the structure, themes, and characters of countless stories, uncovering what made them resonate—or fall flat.

Carrie's analytical skills extend far beyond the world of film. Before and after her time at AFI, she worked with organizations to evaluate and optimize business processes. It was during this work that she discovered how businesses operate much like stories, guided by characters, arcs, and themes that drive their successes or failures. This insight inspired her upcoming book, *Business Rewritten.*

Carrie's academic background also includes a Bachelor of Science in counseling psychology from Penn State University, which deepened her understanding of human behavior. This foundation sharpened her ability to read people—a skill she first developed as a survival mechanism during a challenging childhood. Those experiences taught her how to navigate relationships, find belonging, and ultimately use those lessons to help others.

Carrie's commitment to personal growth is rooted in firsthand experience. She has explored therapy in its many forms—group, individual, psychoanalysis—and has delved into personal growth workshops and metaphysical practices. Her studies in Integrated Body Psychotherapy (IBP), tapping, and hypnotherapy consistently revealed one powerful truth: storytelling is the key to understanding and transforming our lives, even when it's not explicitly named.

Driven by the marvel of human resilience, Carrie believes that if she could turn the pain and challenges of her early years into the life she leads today, then transformation is possible for anyone. *Life Rewritten* is born from her experience, study, and passion for storytelling as a tool for profound change.

Carrie firmly believes we all have the capacity for true happiness. "The pen is in your hand," she says. "Let's begin rewriting your story."

Printed in Dunstable, United Kingdom

67785913R00097